## More Praise for *Burnout to Breakthrough*

"Eileen McDargh provides a clear road map that will give you the inspiration to do more and be more. This book will help you rediscover your passion, unlock your potential, and realize a future filled with unlimited possibilities."

—**Roger Crawford, Hall of Fame Speaker and bestselling author of *How High Can You Bounce?***

"*Burnout to Breakthrough* is a bighearted book, written in a lively style with lots of relatable examples and immediately applicable advice. Eileen McDargh makes reading about a very serious topic extraordinarily engaging and gratifying. It's like having an intimate conversation with a best friend—you know someone's been listening and is there for you. You'll come away with a better sense of what matters most to you and what you can do to reclaim your life."

—**Jim Kouzes, coauthor of *The Leadership Challenge* and Executive Fellow, Center for Innovation and Entrepreneurship, Leavey School of Business, Santa Clara University**

"Eileen McDargh's latest meditation on occupational burnout, *Burnout to Breakthrough*, is a much-needed component to the contemporary dialogue about achieving more by beating burnout and building resilience. By emphasizing the importance of personal leadership elements such as self-talk and energy management, Eileen makes a powerful case for the role of the individual in refueling, recharging, and reclaiming what matters. At the same time, Eileen offers a nuanced, broader perspective about a workplace that is 'preheated' for overachievers, and she equips leaders with valuable questions and practices to help reduce chronic stress among their employees. Eileen's new book is timely, relevant, and highly actionable. Written in her signature buoyant and empowering voice, it's an accessible and empowering read. I highly recommend this as a spiritual companion to my own book, *The Burnout Gamble*."

—**Hamza Khan, cofounder of SkillsCamp**

"Words like *disengagement*, *compassion fatigue*, *burnout*, and even *suicide* exist across industries and generations. In this book, Eileen McDargh offers a powerful and proven formula for building a more positive workplace culture by helping people live more effective and resilient lives."

—**Joe Tye, founder and CEO, Values Coach, and author of *The Florence Prescription***

"You'll be inspired by the wise insights. Buy a book for yourself and a friend. Work through it together as you answer the questions and celebrate your results. You'll be well on your way to breaking through burnout."

—**Sam Horn, author of** *Someday Is Not a Day in the Week*

"Get ready to get energized! From the first sentence, Eileen McDargh captivates you and catapults you into a world of abundance and possibilities. Eileen is the master of energy, and in her brilliant new book, she reveals her secrets. Read *Burnout to Breakthrough* and reap the rewards!"

—**Jesse Lyn Stoner, coauthor of** *Full Steam Ahead!*

"The author knows her stuff. She has been delivering on this topic to organizations around the world. And she lives it! Eileen delivers a very easy-to-digest set of doable ideas that will absolutely move you out of the doldrums and back to delight."

—**Dr. Beverly Kaye, CEO, Bev Kaye & Co., and coauthor of** *Love It, Don't Leave It* **and** *Love 'Em or Lose 'Em*

"Boundlessly brilliant! The answer to our quest to move from burnouts to breakthroughs. Eileen McDargh takes us rapidly from Argh! to Aha! to Ahh. If you are tired of being tired and are seeking to be wiser and stronger and grow through the challenges that keep coming at you, you must get this book. Now!"

—**Bill Jensen, author of the bestsellers** *Simplicity*, *Disrupt!*, **and** *The Courage within Us*

# BURNOUT TO BREAKTHROUGH

# BURNOUT TO BREAKTHROUGH

## BUILDING RESILIENCE TO REFUEL, RECHARGE, AND RECLAIM WHAT MATTERS

## Eileen McDargh

Berrett–Koehler Publishers, Inc.

Berrett-Koehler Publishers, Inc.
1333 Broadway, Suite 1000, Oakland, CA 94612-1921
Tel: (510) 817-2277   Fax: (510) 817-2278   www.bkconnection.com

ORDERING INFORMATION

**Quantity sales.** Special discounts are available on quantity purchases by corporations, associations, and others. For details, contact the "Special Sales Department" at the Berrett-Koehler address above.

**Individual sales.** Berrett-Koehler publications are available through most bookstores. They can also be ordered directly from Berrett-Koehler: Tel: (800) 929-2929; Fax: (802) 864-7626; www.bkconnection.com.

**Orders for college textbook / course adoption use.** Please contact Berrett-Koehler: Tel: (800) 929-2929; Fax: (802) 864-7626.

Distributed to the U.S. trade and internationally by Penguin Random House Publisher Services.

Berrett-Koehler and the BK logo are registered trademarks of Berrett-Koehler Publishers, Inc.

Printed in the United States of America

Berrett-Koehler books are printed on long-lasting acid-free paper. When it is available, we choose paper that has been manufactured by environmentally responsible processes. These may include using trees grown in sustainable forests, incorporating recycled paper, minimizing chlorine in bleaching, or recycling the energy produced at the paper mill.

Library of Congress Cataloging-in-Publication Data

Names: McDargh, Eileen, author.
Title: Burnout to breakthrough : building resilience to refuel, recharge,
  and reclaim what matters / Eileen McDargh.
Description: First edition. | Oakland, CA : Berrett-Koehler Publishers,
  [2020] | Includes bibliographical references and index.
Identifiers: LCCN 2020008985 | ISBN 9781523089468 (paperback) | ISBN
  9781523089482 (epub) | ISBN 9781523089475 (pdf)
Subjects: LCSH: Resilience (Personality trait) | Self-help techniques. |
  Life skills.
Classification: LCC BF698.35.R47 M45 2020 | DDC 158.1–dc23
LC record available at https://lccn.loc.gov/2020008985

First Edition
25 24 23 22 21 20         10 9 8 7 6 5 4 3 2 1

Produced by Wilsted & Taylor Publishing Services
Text design by Nancy Koerner
Copy editing by Nancy Evans
Cover design by Nita Ybarra

*To my GRANDS, Alicia, Clare, Siena, and Keaton,*
*who continue to teach me what matters most*

*To my Sweet William,*
*who refuels my heart every day*

*To my siblings, Susan and John,*
*cohorts in cheers and compassion since the get-go*

# CONTENTS

# BURNOUT TO BREAKTHROUGH

# STOP! LOOK! LISTEN!

It's official. The World Health Organization (WHO) now places burnout in its International Classification of Diseases diagnostic manual. It's no longer just a stress syndrome but rather "a syndrome conceptualized as resulting from chronic workplace stress that has not been successfully managed." It is characterized by three dimensions:

- Feelings of energy depletion or mental exhaustion
- Increased mental distance from one's job or negative feelings toward one's career
- Reduced professional productivity

Let me phrase these dimensions in more common terms. Consider these questions:

- Does the job that turned you on now seem to turn you off?
- Are you working more but enjoying it less?

- Have you lost who you are because you lost the work you loved?

- Does life seem to be leading you rather than you leading a life?

- Are you so exhausted that you can't even sleep?

- Are you struggling to handle the demands of too much to do and too little time?

- Are people telling you that you look tired all the time?

- Have you lost your sense of humor?

- Does it seem that no matter how much you work, there's no completion, no recognition, and little intrinsic or extrinsic reward?

- Do you find yourself short-tempered?

- Are you feeling anxious, unsettled, and circling on a merry-go-round that's no longer merry?

Whether you answered "yes" to one or all of these questions, this book is for you. My intention is to help you not only to "successfully manage" work demands but also to make even larger strides in understanding how to put together a life by design and not by default. In order to recharge, refuel, and reclaim what matters, we need to make a journey of self-discovery. It will require honesty, courage, and a willingness to do exactly what we're warned about at a railroad crossing: *Stop! Look! Listen!* If we don't follow that warning, we can find ourselves flattened by an oncoming locomotive.

You did not consciously choose burnout. No one does.

That's why it's so insidious and, as you will see in chapter 1, you are not alone. This is the Age of Burnout. To be honest, organizational cultures and systems are also to blame for some toxic environments. With that in mind, chapter 3 will offer actions for leaders to take to counteract workplace burnout plus ideas to ensure that an organization breeds well-being, community, and resiliency. I debated long and hard about putting this chapter first because you, the reader, might find this a reason to point to the organization and say, "See, I told you so." You might cross your arms and wait for the organization to change. Don't do that! Share the chapter as appropriate, but start working on YOU!

My primary intention is to put you in command, to have you take control of what you put in your twenty-four-hour day.

- First, you'll explore what *burnout* is, what its symptoms are, and what the potential triggers are that ignite the "flames."

- Second, you will learn to stop, look, and listen deeply to what is happening in the critical parts of your life. What really is going on? What are you doing, saying, or thinking that is exhausting your mental and physical energies? This is *breakout*—the understanding—the "Aha" moment.

- Third, you will discover that *breakthrough* comes when we break out of energy-draining thoughts, feelings, and behaviors and consider more powerful options to refuel, recharge, and reclaim what matters. That's breakthrough! Ahhhh.

Breakthrough comes when you build resilience skillsets and mindsets and realign energy flows. Yes, energy! That's really what this is all about. Energy is the core of resilience. Resilience is *not* about "bouncing back," as the dictionary insists. Rather, for humans, it's about growing through this period of our life to a better place. Building resilience is like building a muscle. It takes persistence and patience. With use, it becomes easier for us to refuel, recharge, and reclaim what matters. This is not an overnight process. It takes time.

I'll also offer a series of options to move you across the track and into breakthrough. I'll explore four sources that hold the possibility of giving us energy or depleting our energy. These are:

**HEAD** Our thinking affects all aspects of our energy.

**HEART** Emotions rule our actions and our relationships.

**HANDS** In addition to thinking and feeling, doing creates real power. Carl Jung said, "Often the hands will solve a mystery that the intellect has struggled with in vain."

**HUMOR** Life needs laughter and the perspective of humor.

## DON'T LOOK FOR BALANCE

Note that word *breakthrough*. Breakthrough is not "balance."

Who are we trying to kid? There's no such thing as balance. This is why I have objected to the term "balance" as the end goal for people experiencing burnout—although I admit in my earlier work, I was guilty of using that term. If I asked you to hold up your hands to show me what balance looks like, inevitably you would hold up your hands in some replica of the scales of justice, with the implication that balance means equality.

Wouldn't it be nice if everything in our home and work life demanded equal attention, delivered equal rewards, and prompted an equal feeling of well-being and calm? Our energy could be equally distributed. Alas! Life is never going to be "equal." Let's get real here. The very word "balance" conjures up an image that sets up a false expectation and is not sustainable. Stuff happens.

Breakthrough, however, happens when our energy is consciously distributed to what REALLY matters most *at this specific period of our life*. At different periods of our life, what matters most will change and energy requirements will shift. Our task is to consciously realign our energy flow so we can recharge and refuel.

> There are years that ask questions and years that answer.
>
> —ZORA NEALE HURSTON

We move into burnout when we don't make that shift, when our energy is exhausted at the expense of other parts of our life. In this book, you'll read stories of folks who did not make the shift and became fried into the bargain.

## WE LEARN FROM OTHERS

I'm grateful for the people who candidly shared their burn-out stories with me. You might recognize yourself in their stories. In some cases, their names have been changed for privacy, but their experiences, insights, and admitted challenges are all real. And I use their exact words—some pretty graphic—to honestly report their experience.

## HOW TO USE THIS BOOK

Whether you picked this book up for yourself, a friend, your spouse, or your team, my hope is that you'll find answers here to help you craft a life and a workplace that nurtures and supports your best self. Please take your time. I ask many questions that invite intro-spection and reflection. You might decide to read with a notebook at hand. Be warned: I am a huge be-liever in the power of putting pen to paper. Recent studies from psychologists and neurosci-entists alike have found that writing by hand boosts your ability to retain information, comprehend new ideas, and be more productive.[1] Get a journal and make notations as you read.

> I write to discover what I know.
>
> —FLANNERY O'CONNOR

The activities in this book are designed to help you iden-tify where more powerful, energy-enhancing choices might be made. You didn't pick up this book because something happened yesterday. The good news is that building resil-ience and the ability to respond in more powerful ways to potential burnout scenarios in our life can be learned. You will find ways to move from burnout to breakthrough and

**Caveat.** Some events in our life may leave us with post-traumatic stress disorder (PTSD), which can require medical attention and psychotherapy. On the flip side, there is also PTG—post-traumatic growth. According to the Posttraumatic Growth Research Group at the University of North Carolina at Charlotte, PTG can be understood as positive change resulting from an individual's struggle with a major life crisis or traumatic event.[2] This book does not address PTSD or PTG. My focus is on helping organizations and individuals deal with the stresses of everyday life and work and to cultivate resiliency while learning to refuel, recharge, and reclaim what matters.

The best resource I have found with expertise in the full continuum of trauma, resiliency, and post-traumatic growth is the nonprofit National Resilience Institute. Their working definition of resiliency is "the capacity to prepare for, adapt to, and grow through trauma, disruption, or loss." Dr. Mollie Marti, the founding CEO of the Institute, emphasizes that many skills that help grow resiliency are teachable. She notes that research shows that post-traumatic stress symptoms and post-traumatic growth are not on opposite ends of a spectrum, but rather can coexist over time as people make meaning of their experiences. For more resources, visit the National Resilience Institute at http://www.NationalResilienceInstitute.org.

refuel, recharge, and reclaim what matters. Consider this your blueprint, your diagram, for moving from burnout to breakout to breakthrough by building your resilience muscle to refuel, recharge, and reclaim what matters.

Let's get going!

# PART 1

# BURNOUT

## CHAPTER 1

BURNOUT

# THE AGE OF BURNOUT

*The more things change,*
*the more some things remain the same...*

—ANONYMOUS

What the heck is going on??? In the past two years, I've been asked to present to a wide variety of organizations and audiences on the topics of overcoming burnout and building resilience. While I have lectured in this area for years, never have I had so many requests for these specific topics!

From student leaders in a major engineering college to literally thousands of pharmacists at an annual convention; from patient safety advocates to oncology nurses; from executive women to IT professionals preparing for a huge buyout; from an international women's conference on disruption to coaching professionals in Manila—it's all the same cry: HELP!

I wrote my first book years ago in order to understand my own burnout. So, in some ways, this feels like déjà vu—but bigger and meaner.

**WHERE IT ALL BEGAN**

My story: In 1984, I was prompted to write my first book, *Work for a Living & Still Be Free to Live!*, because I frankly hated my job, was exhausted to the max trying to appease a demanding manager, and was just plain miserable. A burned-out and unhappy camper, to be sure. I discovered I was not alone. Colleagues wanted to know how I did it—I just closed up my tent and left without anything in the offing to pay bills. (This is called walking out on faith!) They, too, were miserable and wanted to leave their respective positions.

I discovered the work of Dr. Herbert Freudenberger, a psychologist who introduced the term "burnout" into our vocabulary in 1974 and then wrote *Burn Out: How to Beat the High Cost of Success.*[1] He defined burnout as "To deplete oneself. To exhaust one's physical and mental resources. To wear oneself out by excessively striving to reach some unrealistic expectation imposed by one's self or the values of society." My expectation had been that I had to stay in a job that depleted my energy.

That surely was part of what I was experiencing—except there was more. I was engaged in work that had no intrinsic meaning for me. It took me almost three decades to realize that a lack of purposeful work can also lead to the very exhaustion Freudenberger described. This was what my colleagues some forty years ago were also experiencing. Be warned, however: Freudenberger also insisted that a state of fatigue can be brought about by "devotion to a cause, a way of life, or relationship that failed to produce the expected reward." In short, he believed that underachievers would not necessarily experience burnout, but rather committed idealists, who set unrealistically high goals and whose energy was directed to only one part of life, would.

Unfortunately, the concept of "burnout," as explored at the time by Dr. Freudenberger and Dr. Christina Maslach, a social psychologist and creator of the Maslach Burnout Inventory,[2] was initially dismissed as pseudoscience. It was also relegated to the realms of the helping professions and found only in connection to this thing we call "work."

Big mistake. Today, almost four decades later, burnout has become BIG stuff, with the "blaze" becoming uglier and more intense. The Maslach Burnout Inventory is now the most widely accepted and used measurement tool for burnout. The definition of burnout has been expanded to include the exhaustion of physical or emotional strength or motivation, usually as a result of prolonged stress or frustration.[3]

### THIS IS A GLOBAL EPIDEMIC

Consider these statistics:

#### NORTH AMERICA

- The cost of stress and burnout to North American companies is estimated to range between $120 and $300 billion.[4]

- 58 percent of working Canadians report excessive stress every day at work.

- One US study found that work stress contributed to 120,000 deaths per year.

- *Psychology Today* (May 2019) reported that physician and health care provider burnout in the United States has reached epidemic proportions, with close to 50 percent identifying symptoms.[5]

- Burnout is responsible for up to half of all employee attrition. Employees are working more hours for little to no additional pay, recognition, or a sense of appreciation. Hence, they are searching for new jobs.

### AUSTRALIA

- $34 billion is spent every year on burnout incidents.

- In 2013, the Australian Medical Students' Association (AMSA) found that about one-third of all university students reported suffering from anxiety, harmful drinking, or eating disorders due to financial stress.

- Up to 75 percent of clergy suffer from work stress and 25 percent have reported stress leave or burnout.[6]

### EUROPE

- In Europe, health professionals and educators experience the highest levels of burnout. In Germany, the epidemic resulted in the creation of the musical, *Das BurnOut*!

- A recent EU Labour Force Survey found that a quarter of the respondents—55.6 million workers—said their well-being had been affected by risks such as too much work, long hours, tight deadlines, and organizational changes.[7]

**AFRICA**

- Work-related stress and major depression, burnout, and anxiety disorders are costing South Africa's economy an estimated R40.6 billion a year—equivalent to 2.2 percent of the country's gross domestic product.[8]

- Maternal health staff found that 72 percent of workers suffer from emotional exhaustion.

- More than 75 percent of nurses in South Africa report fatigue, sadness, low energy, and frustration.

**EAST ASIA**

- Bloomberg Report stated that Chinese media states that about 600,000 Chinese a year die from working too hard.[9]

- Japan has even coined a word for death by burnout: *karoshi*. Government officials reveal that one out of every five workers is at risk for overwork. And there is also a word for suicide related to overwork: *karojisatsu*. For proven cases of either type of death, the government awards around $20,000 to victims' families, and employers can pay up to $1 million in damages.

**INDIA**

- One out of every five employees of the company India Inc. is suffering from workplace depression, says a new survey, and medical experts blame it on a lack of support systems in both the workplace and personal circles.[10]

I could offer article after article about "burnout." Just do a Google news search for this word, and you'll find more than enough data to convince you that you are not alone. While you are looking, check out articles on "suicide." Suicide rates are the highest they have been in the United States in three decades. Depression is at an all-time high. Even more frightening, students in high school and college are reporting anxiety, overwork, fear, and mental health challenges.

As I stated in the Introduction, in May 2019, the World Health Organization (WHO) globally legitimized "burnout" by including it in the latest version of its International Statistical Classification of Diseases and Related Health Problems.[11] They are quite careful to call it an occupational phenomenon. It is not classified as a medical condition.

### A CAVEAT TO THE WORLD HEALTH ORGANIZATION'S DEFINITION

The WHO did not go far enough. It categorized burnout as a work-related hazard. In reality, there can be times when the workplace is our place of refuge because the demands in the rest of our life are enormous. Emotional and physical exhaustion can occur when caring for an aging parent, juggling the demands of school and work, or working through a divorce. Such times require more conscious choices for self-care. You might find yourself in this stage.

### SO, GIVEN THE GLOBAL NATURE OF BURNOUT, HOW DO YOU STACK UP?

The following is a short survey I've compiled. (You'll find a list of various and longer assessments in the Resources.)

# BURNOUT ASSESSMENT

Fill out the number that best describes your behavior.

*1. Never  2. Seldom  3. Sometimes  4. Frequently  5. Always*

1. I tire more easily than I used to.
   I feel fatigued rather than energetic.      \_\_\_\_\_

2. I find optimism a hard thing
   to come by.      \_\_\_\_\_

3. I seem to be working harder but
   accomplishing less.      \_\_\_\_\_

4. I have a hard time asking for help,
   believing I *should* do things
   on my own.      \_\_\_\_\_

5. I find myself short-tempered
   and irritable.      \_\_\_\_\_

6. I am uncomfortable challenging
   the status quo and taking risks.      \_\_\_\_\_

7. I find myself "overdoing": food, drugs,
   or alcohol.      \_\_\_\_\_

8. I can't remember the last time I played.      \_\_\_\_\_

9. I find it hard to laugh at myself.      \_\_\_\_\_

10. I can't find time to do routine things
    like reading, sending out cards, or
    making my bed.                                    _____

11. I think meditation is for monks
    and I'm too busy for it.                          _____

12. My body is experiencing more
    physical complaints than normal.                  _____

13. I often feel alone and unappreciated
    for what I do.                                    _____

14. The only regular exercise I get is
    walking to and from the parking lot.              _____

15. I have a hard time concentrating
    and often procrastinate.                          _____

                                        TOTAL    _____

Please add up your numbers and see where you line up. Remember, this is a just a small sample survey and does not take into account the current context of your work and life. But it will give you some food for thought.

60–75 . . . Ummm, don't get too close to anything that's flammable. You might become a crispy critter.

45–59 . . . Keep reading this book. You still have work to do to keep your life/work from igniting.

30–44 . . . You have some days that are diamonds and some days that are stone. Let's see what actions can give you more diamonds.

15–29 . . . You get to write the next book or join me on a podcast. You have figured this out.

# WHAT TRIGGERS THE FLAMES?

*Exhaustion is not a badge of honor.*
— BRENÉ BROWN

How did we get to this place?

Our lives are not compartmentalized into neat boxes labeled "work," "home," "family," "friends," "community," "school," "health," "religious institutions," and "associations." We dance among these entities, often weaving parts of one into another. Caring for an aging parent does not stop while working at one's desk. Serving as the president of a local nonprofit does not disappear while meeting a work demand. Studying for final exams does not isolate one from the physical need to exercise and sleep.

To begin the journey from burnout to breakthrough, it's necessary to *stop* and consciously examine all facets of our life. Now, I admit to being a jerk—a knee jerk. I respond instantly to what I think needs to be fixed. Alas, I am often off the mark. Some of you might be the opposite—procrastinators. You wait for things to simmer down before taking action. That can also prove to be an unhealthy response. Instead, let's blend the two reactions and explore more deeply. This will lead us into breakout.

Five triggers might contribute to burnout:

1. Personal history and "voices"

2. Technology tyrants

3. Disconnected connections

4. Caretaker crisis

5. Lack of meaning and purpose

For now, just reflect on whether any of these "triggers" might be simmering in various parts of your life. Honestly owning the presence of any of these triggers can be one of your breakout steps toward breakthrough. Consider this a diagnostic chapter that lays out possible contributing factors.

## TRIGGER #1

### PERSONAL HISTORY AND "VOICES"

I had the wonderful opportunity to be on a program with Hamza Khan, a marvelous millennial and author of *The Burnout Gamble*.[1] He calls himself a recovering overachiever, and his wonderful book is the result of burning out in a major fashion. The son of immigrants from India, Hamza needed to achieve results and prove his worth to his parents, which netted him names like "robot" and "machine." A three-day stretch with less than an hour of combined sleep found him passed out on a bathroom floor, out cold for twelve hours in a pool of vomit!

He didn't take the warning seriously. The voices in his

head and his high ego need for wild success continued. You'll have to read his book to get the entire story about his final wake-up call. However, his dramatic flameout was the product of stress brought on by trying to excel in anything he touched *and* trying to live up to the "superstar" image perceived by his family and the world.

Gen Xer Lin Jackson, today a senior manager in a major biotech company, recalls that her journey into burnout began like the proverbial frog in boiling water. At age seventeen, she went to high school in the morning, worked at a co-op on data processing in the afternoon, and then was sent out as a third-party consultant. Three jobs! Lin explained that she came from a lower-middle-class family. Her father instilled in her two things to get ahead: education and hard work! Lots of both. "He wanted me to have a different life and I was to be the first generation to earn that life. I listened to his voice . . . for decades."

While your internal voice might not be as strident and demanding as Hamza's or Lin's, we all have voices that talk to us about who we are and who we can be.

These voices can also be powerful and positive. Tina Turner, born Anna Mae Bullock, was raised by her sharecropper grandparents in Nutbush, Tennessee. I can't help but think that the voices telling her to never stop singing propelled her from poverty and an abusive marriage into her title as "The Queen of Rock and Roll."

**QUESTIONS**

What do your voices say to you? Is it true?

Is it what you believe and want in your deepest soul?

What is the price you pay and is it worth it?

## TRIGGER #2
### TECHNOLOGY TYRANTS

How many of us jump when a text message dings? Or stop what we are doing to answer the latest email that flashes across our screen? Multitasking is a myth, having us believe we are being productive when actually we are not.

A *Wall Street Journal* video, "How Smart Phones Sabotage Your Brain's Ability to Focus," noted that some researchers suggest that heavy multitaskers are 40 percent less productive.[2] This means that one must work longer and harder to regain focus. Talk about stress!

In another study, Stanford University researcher Clifford Nass found that people who were considered heavy multitaskers were actually worse at sorting out relevant information from irrelevant details.[3] This finding is particularly surprising because it was assumed that heavy multitaskers would actually be better at this kind of sorting. But that wasn't the only problem these heavy multitaskers faced. They also showed greater difficulty when it came to switching from one task to another and they were much less mentally organized. Smart phones can make us dumb and email can wreck our ability to focus.

## QUESTIONS

Do you consider yourself a multitasking genius?

Are you addicted to your smart phone?

Do you have a hard time "shutting off" at the end of a day?

Can you limit your to-do list to what is actually feasible in a day?

Do you compete in the "my list-is-longer-than-your list" race?

# TRIGGER #3
## DISCONNECTED CONNECTIONS

The third trigger is also catalyzed by technology. On a college campus, I watched students walking, their heads bent to look at text messages or email. Never once did they stop to interact. I sat by a reflecting pool outside a major hospital where medical personnel were taking a break. But no one was talking. Again, all eyes were focused on their phones. Standing in line at the grocery store, I found myself starting to pull out my phone to read email rather than smiling at the person behind me and saying good morning to the clerk. Shame on me!

The March 20, 2019, edition of *Scientific American* revealed that a recent study found that a staggering 47 percent of Americans often feel alone, left out and lacking meaningful connection with others.[4] This is true for all ages, from teenagers to older adults. The number of people who perceive themselves to be alone, isolated, or distant from others has reached epidemic levels in both the United States and other parts of the world. From the UK to Japan and Australia, governments are taking notice. Loneliness has been estimated to shorten a person's life by fifteen years, equivalent in impact to being obese or smoking fifteen cigarettes per day.[5] A recent study revealed a surprising association between loneliness and cancer mortality risk, pointing to the role loneliness plays in cancer's course, including responsiveness to treatments. Not surprisingly, loneliness causes stress—the catalyst for burnout.

While we can't blame loneliness solely on technology, the reality is that the more we automate and turn to technology before people, the less human contact we end up with.

People are stressed, and human connection is the remedy. As the director of nursing at an oncology hospital told me, "These young nurses have medical skills but zero idea how to talk to patients and their families. They are burning out because they don't know how to talk to these patients. It's now become a training issue for us!"

## TRIGGER #4
### CARETAKER CRISIS

Life happens. With an aging population, many of us will experience the need to care for aging parents in various stages of physical and mental decline. We can be caught between parents and children. Or a loved one might suffer a debilitating illness and need your attention. Self-care gets pushed to the last item on your list.

Managers, take a clue from former surgeon general Dr. Vivek Murthy, who wrote a fascinating cover story for the *Harvard Business Review*.[6] Dr. Murthy will not only convince you that creating workplace connections is good for business but he also offers specific actions that allow groups to actually know and value each other. Forget mandatory fun and traditional "team building." Murthy suggests that a connected workforce is more likely to enjoy greater fulfillment, productivity, and engagement while being protected from burnout.

Dr. Murthy created "Inside Scoop," an exercise in which team members are asked to share something about themselves through pictures for five minutes during staff meetings. This is an eye-opener that generates greater insights and allows colleagues to learn about one another's personal lives.

Strong social connections show that positive emotions improve performance and resilience. Make strengthening social connections a strategic priority (and this is not done through team games). Encourage coworkers to reach out and help others—and to accept that help.

## TRIGGER #5
### LACK OF MEANING AND PURPOSE

In a classic story, two bricklayers are working on a church in Europe. A passerby asks the men what they are doing. One bricklayer responds, "Can't you see? I am laying bricks." The other bricklayer, smiling widely, says, "I am building a cathedral!"

An old tale, to be sure, but today it is more powerful

than ever. The first man shrugged off his work as just a task. The second man saw his work as a contribution to something greater than himself: a cathedral.

In her powerful, evidenced-based book, *The Power of Meaning: Finding Fulfillment in a World Obsessed with Happiness*, Emily Esfahani Smith outlines the connection between a lack of meaning and depression, burnout, and suicide.[7] Happiness is equated not with having wealth but rather with being engaged in finding something worthwhile to do with one's time—something that is meaningful. This doesn't mean being able to cure cancer or achieve global peace, but rather working at something that has significance beyond a paycheck. If your work is stale, plodding, and without personal meaning, burnout might not be far off.

Consider this classic experiment conducted in the 1970s by researchers Ellen Langer and Judith Rodin. The elderly residents of a nursing home were each given a houseplant. One group was told that the staff would care for their plant. The other residents were given the job of caring for the plant themselves. At the end of eighteen months, the residents who cared for their own plant were remarkably better than the other group.[8]

I'm not suggesting you find a potted African violet. However, in subsequent chapters you'll find people who brought an extra something special to their work that felt like a contribution. In chapter 9, you'll meet a hospital housekeeper who uses her art to liven up the hospital floor and the patients.

# THE ORGANIZATION'S ROLE IN BURNOUT

*Sometimes I wish I just had a summer job here.*

—JOHN F. KENNEDY,
TO STUDENTS IN WASHINGTON, D.C.

Interesting, isn't it—even a position that someone spends years and a fortune to attain is not always what it's cracked up to be. While there are downsides and upsides to any position, the workplace environment deserves closer attention. In the Introduction, I promised to look at the organizational factors that prompt burnout conditions: specifically, leader behaviors and cultural conditioning.

For those of you who are managers in your organization, it's time to do an honest evaluation. As you read this, consider the questions I pose. Maybe it's time to break out from outmoded ways of thinking, feeling, and acting in order to break through to create a workplace that allows people to refuel, recharge, and reclaim what matters! And if you are not in a leadership position, perhaps you'll consider sharing this chapter with your manager!

### LEADERS DRIVE PEOPLE TO BURNOUT

"Wait," you say! "We have all these wellness programs in place. We have nap rooms and yoga classes and we provide smoking cessation programs." That's a start, but it's not enough. Corporate spending on workplace wellness programs is estimated at $50 billion globally and is expected to grow 7 percent annually to 2025. Yet according to the National Institute of Mental Health, workplace wellness programs have failed to improve people's health or change their work experience.[1]

The reason? Wellness programs put the onus on the employee instead of acknowledging that the employer might be part of the problem. In the book *Building Resilience for Success*,[2] the authors do a great job of listing workplace practices that push people over the top and into burnout. How many of these practices are present in your workplace?

RESOURCES AND COMMUNICATION: Infrequent feedback and communication; inadequate training; out-of-date technology and equipment.

CONTROL: Ideas not listened to; lack of control over job and decisions; performance goals imposed rather than created collaboratively.

WORKLOAD: Unreasonable expectations; too little time to complete tasks; work unreasonably interfering with home life.

JOB SECURITY AND CHANGE: Job insecurity; fear of skill redundancy; change for the sake of change.

WORK RELATIONSHIPS: Aggressive management style; others taking credit for your success; isolation and/or lack of support.

JOB CONDITIONS: Inequality in pay and benefits; dull, repetitive work; difficult customers.

**QUESTIONS**

Does this sound like your organization?

What would it take for you to speak out and identify where you might impact change?

OVERLOADING MEETINGS AND EMAILS: In too many organizations, the corporate culture requires meetings upon meetings, often involving people who do not need to be there or with content that could have been handled by a phone call or a simple email (sent *only* to the people who need to see it). Not everyone has to "become aligned" or sign off. And emails alone often stand for escalation and error. The average frontline supervisor devotes about eight hours each week to sending, reading, and answering emails—many of which should never have been sent.

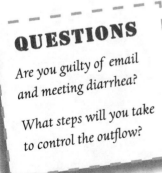

**QUESTIONS**

Are you guilty of email and meeting diarrhea?

What steps will you take to control the outflow?

OVERLOADING TALENT WITH TOO MUCH WORK: How many times have I heard employees say that the organization was downsized but the workload never changed! Capable employees are inundated, and too often no one stopped to question if the "work" was really efficient and required. There's too much redundancy. I hear a common refrain, "But we have new technology." Often that poses an even bigger time drain, particularly if there's no work-around during a learning curve.

Overworking is the norm, with little time-management discipline. It's not only the volume of work that pushes people into burnout but also the unwritten expectation that employees must be constantly "on" even when they are at home in the evening or on the weekends. Additionally, many executives have no idea how long work activities actually take and whether those activities really add value at the end of the day.

## QUESTIONS

Have you asked your team what activities seem to be redundant and/or senseless? Trust me, they will give you an answer.

Are you courageous enough to push upward and identify what activities are really necessary?

Where are you guilty of striking the proverbial match?

What are you willing to do to influence your organization's culture?

Is your management style to blame?

KEEPING DIFFICULT MANAGERS AND INCOMPETENT EMPLOYEES IN PLACE: I remember leaving an organization—finally—after I had had enough of working for a vice president who screamed at her staff, took credit for other people's work, and demanded fealty despite her incompetence. But I was lucky. I had fortunately lined up a job before I turned in my resignation. Others were not so graced.

Incompetent employees can also be a drain on the team. I've seen what happens to engagement when there is no proper feedback or remediation. Ignoring the situation or passing that employee along to another department is not only foolish but also unfair to all involved.

### A VARIATION ON THIS THEME FOR LEADERS— WHAT POSITIVE ACTIONS TO TAKE

Another way to explore how your organization can create an environment that supports employee well-being is an exercise recommended by leadership guru Jim Collins, author of *Good to Great*.[3] He calls it the Mars Group.

Collins asks a group of fifty to sixty people to imagine they are recreating the best attributes of their organization on another planet. (For our purposes, you'd want attributes for employee well-being.) The trick is that there are seats for only five to seven people on the rocket ship. In Collins's experience, those selected are invariably a powerful, credible group because they live those attributes. When this group reports back, leaders will have a roadmap for creating or strengthening the organizational culture in relation to controlling burnout and building resilience to refuel and recharge.

### CONSIDER A GROSS PROGRAM

Doctors, nurses, and clinicians report massive rates of burnout. Hawaii Pacific Health created an initiative, the Get Rid of Stupid Stuff (GROSS) program, through which personnel are asked to identify work that does not add value—such as documentation that does not need to be routine or could be done in a more efficient manner. This program was described in the *New England Journal of Medicine* in November 2018, and GROSS went viral.[4]

### WHEN EMPLOYEES DEFINE
### A COMPANY'S CULTURE

The advertising agency 22squared recognized that an always-on culture can result in high turnover. According to Chris Tuff, partner at the agency, employees are offered five days off every year to volunteer for the community. After three years, they can give one month of their time, all expenses paid, to a nonprofit anywhere in the world. Tuff says employees are empowered to define the culture on their own terms and he often hears that 22squared's culture is a major factor in why people have chosen to work for them. Meetings are also device-free to encourage a focused, collaborative environment.[5]

Check out Instagram at hashtag #22Culture. You'll see almost 4,000 posts of happy people, babies, parties, and Tuff's book, *The Millennial Whisperer.*

### WHAT YOU CAN DO NOW IF YOU ARE
### NOT IN A LEADERSHIP POSITION

If you are now feeling discouraged about your organization because you are not in a leadership position, please stop. I know it's much easier to blame the organization, our genes, the cycle of the moon, our parents, the 1 percent, and anything else you'd like to put into the fire. Moving from burnout to breakthrough requires an honest evaluation that, depending upon your current situation, can be an easy exercise or a challenging exorcism.

But as you will read in subsequent chapters, you are not powerless. You do have choices. You have a sphere of influence. And you have the ability to discover what Shawn Achor calls the Happiness Advantage.[6] Achor has taught his seven principles of positive psychology to companies worldwide—companies like KPMG and UBS—with the result that employees learned how to become more engaged, motivated, resilient, and productive through retraining their brains to see patterns of possibilities. I'll share more of Achor's wisdom in chapter 9.

If you haven't done so, please go back and look at the triggers and the questions I posed at the start of chapter 2. Write out your responses—either in real time on real—gasp—paper, or type them into the note section of your smart phone. Don't want to write? Then talk your answers into your phone. You'll want to look at them again.

# THE ROLE OF RESILIENCE

*The human capacity for burden is like bamboo—far more flexible than you'd ever believe at first glance.*

—JODI PICOULT, *MY SISTER'S KEEPER*

### THROW OUT THE DICTIONARY

If I ask *any* person to give me a simple definition of resiliency, the answer is always "bounce back." That is certainly on the mark for the first definition by Merriam-Webster: "The ability of something to return to its original size and shape after being compressed or deformed."

This works just fine if you are a piece of steel, a willow tree, or a sofa cushion—but not if you are a human being. When we experience the compression of stress or an event that knocks us down, we are forever changed. You either stay down or you grow through it. There is no going back. As the Greek philosopher Heraclitus (born ca. 544 BC) said,

"No man ever steps in the same river twice for it's not the same river and he's not the same man."

The second definition is also not accurate for our human experience: "An ability to recover from or adjust easily to adversity or change." A few things are wrong with this definition. First, the word "recover" implies that something went wrong. "Adjust easily" is a lovely thought, but in many cases, adjusting is hard work and not easy. And lastly, this definition implies that resiliency only kicks into gear in the face of adversity or change.

### TRY THE *HUMAN* DEFINITION

Here's my definition: Resiliency is *growing* through challenge or opportunity, so you end up wiser and stronger. As the Japanese say, "Get knocked down seven times, get up eight." Resiliency ultimately means managing your energy so that you have the mental, emotional, physical, and spiritual hardiness to get up and move forward. What is energy but the ability to do work! You also need energy if you have an incredible opportunity. You need energy to run your career, to handle your household, to throw a party, to raise your kids, or to plan a funeral.

Breakout happens when we reach an "Aha moment" in understanding that how we think, feel, and act influences our energy. Breakthrough will only come, however, if we realize we must make a change to realign our energy. That creates our Ahhhh. Building resilience is the next step for increasing our energy resources, and for *creating connections* that support and renew our energy to handle what matters most at this particular period of our lives.

Consider a power grid. Energy flows through the grid if the connections are good. Consider a car. Turn the engine on and, if the connections are good, a spark flies from the battery and the car moves. Bad connections, no movement. In short, energy is either generated through good connections or dissipated through poor connections. I'll borrow from Einstein's equation of $E = mc^2$. In my model, Energy equals Meaningful Connections to the power of two. The "two" can be you and another person, an event, a cause, or your soul! Meaningful connections create energy!

We create or lose energy by how we connect with our *head* (what we are thinking), our *heart* (what we are feeling), and our *hands* (what we are doing). Energy is also generated by *humor* and by *meaning*. The latter is a belief that when one is engaged in meaningful work that matters and leaves a legacy—no matter how large or small—the energy to continue grows.

Are you beginning to see the correlation with burnout? All definitions of burnout are about exhaustion, zero energy, an inability to savor life, unhappiness, depression, and withdrawal. But sometimes we're slow to get the breakout Ahas. We're slow to realize where our energy is being depleted.

Let me give you a personal example. As newlyweds, we were an instant family: my precious husband came with a ready-made family ranging in ages from ten to nineteen. While son Todd could be on his own in a rental unit, the two girls were with us—blessedly so. My energy became focused on doing everything I could to make this family unit work: from family dinners every night to special spur-of-the-moment outings; from making sure that the house had order and cleanliness to having healthy food in the pantry and refrigerator; from taking special time to talk and listen to my girls to laughing with my Sweet William.

Bill had a consulting assignment that took him away 5.5 days of the week. At the same time, I had launched my own business and was trying to get it up and running along with being a first-time mother. Sleep became a sometime thing and exercise consisted of running up and down grocery aisles. Although I had successfully taught a couple hundred children from ages eight to sixteen, living with them was a whole other thing—particularly when the parent whom they adored was absent so much.

Just writing this memory brings up my stress levels. My Ahas came by fits and starts. A couple of breakouts here and there. I connected with my head to really ask myself what I was thinking and saying inside my head and whether it gave me energy or drained my energy. I realized I didn't have to be perfect. Being me was enough. I had to develop heart courage to firmly ask for the support I needed from Bill. I got into action and went to family counseling. And I learned what work assignments I could do without killing myself in the bargain. I learned to say no. I was beginning to build a muscle for resiliency that led from my various Ahas to the wonderful Ahhhh of celebrating an incredible family.

### ANOTHER WAY TO THINK ABOUT STRESS

Think of burnout and resiliency like the double helix found within our DNA. Resiliency can be intertwined with the complex and multifaceted events of our life. Stress is not always a bad thing. It is our body and mind's reaction to changes that can be demanding. There's a difference between *eustress*, which is positive, and *distress*, which is negative. Handling both types of stress requires energy, that is, resiliency!

According to psychologists, eustress is motivating and uses focused energy. It's exciting and provides the ability to handle and improve performance. Consider an athlete who is getting ready to run a race. He's trained for this. He's ready and he is experiencing eustress. It's also short-term. Once the race is over, eustress goes away. I now look for work that affords eustress.

Distress, however, causes anxiety and concern and decreases performance. It's unpleasant and thought to be outside our coping abilities. It can be short- or long-term and can lead to physical or mental problems. Consider the athlete who is a long-distance runner. Suddenly, the coach tells him that he will compete in the high jump the next day. He has never done this. He is untrained. Once he hears that news, he's going to develop a migraine, throw up, or head to the nearest bar!

### CAN RESILIENCE BE LEARNED?

The next obvious question is this: Is resiliency genetic? Aren't there people who just have more grit, energy, and resiliency? After amassing twenty years of research, Dr. Stephen Southwick and Dr. Dennis Charney released their findings in their book *Resilience: The Science of Mastering Life's Greatest Challenges*. They concluded: "Some people genetically appear to be more resilient because they do have a more rapid firing of neurons into the pre-frontal cortex."[1] Think of the prefrontal cortex as the seat of executive functioning. It acts as a conductor for other parts of the brain and moderates complex cognitive behavior, social behavior, and decision-making. The more quickly neurons fire in this area of the brain, the more quickly a person responds to events.

Here's the good news: Southwick and Charney concluded that people can be trained to be more resilient. Our neurobiological systems are highly adaptive. Thanks to the brain's neuroplasticity, neurons in the prefrontal cortex can rewire with practice, patience, and persistence.

### THE POWER OF A GROWTH MINDSET
### VERSUS A FIXED MINDSET

Well-renowned Stanford psychologist Carol Dweck, author of *Mindset: The New Psychology of Success*,[2] has successfully proven that developing a growth mindset versus a fixed mindset can create not only a love of learning but also a resilience when faced with a challenge or what seems like a setback. You can catch yourself operating from a fixed mindset that closes off possibilities and instead work on seeing multiple options.

Dweck relates the example of Christopher Reeve, the actor who was thrown from a horse and became completely paralyzed from the neck down. His growth mindset refused to accept what appeared to be inevitable. Reeve started a demanding exercise program that, despite the pessimism of doctors, resulted in him beginning to regain movement after five years. He was far from cured, but brain scans showed that he was sending signals to parts of his body, so movement was beginning in his hands, arms, legs, and torso. He stretched his abilities and in doing so also opened the potential of hope for others with spinal cord injuries. Tragically, he died of cardiac arrest as a reaction to a drug he was given for sepsis. But his inspiration and model of a growth mindset remain!

People with a growth mindset stretch themselves and relish challenge. Over time, you can literally create new patterns of thinking and acting, creating new neural pathways that are more life enhancing. I think of this process as cultivating resiliency. Training your brain to learn new patterns to handle the stresses of life is not done in one sitting. Much like a garden, you cultivate. You must loosen the soil, plant seeds, water the seeds, feed the seeds, and weed out what is choking out the new behavior.

## ORGANIZATIONAL RESILIENCE

I define organizational resilience as growing through opportunity or challenge and becoming wiser and stronger as an entity. This doesn't necessarily mean bigger. Rather, think of this as being more focused on encouraging innovation, allowing employees to grow and develop their unique skills, and operating from a desire to connect in meaningful ways with all stakeholders. I identify resilient organizations as those that have a firm grasp on reality, a deep belief in shared values that transcend profit, a way to make meaning out of hardships, and an ability to improvise as needed. The list of now defunct companies who failed to change or existed solely to line the pockets of a few is telling. Resilient organizations have growth mindsets versus fixed mindsets.

# PART 2

# BREAKOUT

## CHAPTER 5

**BREAKOUT**

# YOUR BODY

*Insanity is doing the same thing over and over again*
*but expecting different results.*

— ALBERT EINSTEIN

A breakout is an insight that gives you a moment of Aha! Breakout stops you in your tracks and prods you forward. You think a little more carefully, studying something more deeply. There might be hints followed by guesses. With enough breakouts you move from Aha to Ahhhh. That's breakthrough!

STOP first. LOOK next. LISTEN deeply.

### START WITH YOUR PHYSICAL BODY

Your body often outsmarts your brain! It will tell you, if you listen, that your energy resources are running only on fumes and you need to reconsider your actions. Here is a case in point.

David and his wife were scheduled to have dinner with us on Sunday, a date established months before. Alas, three days before our gathering, David sent us a picture of his face and an email that said he'd have to cancel. His face was covered in hives and the doctor was running tests. The doctor said it was a food allergy exacerbated by stress.

As David explained, "There's simply a great deal on my plate of late, including multiple projects at work, over-committed on my volunteer work, and contemplating impending retirement. Typically, I keep my head down and power through such periods, but this time it's different."

If David had stopped long enough, he might have asked himself whether these hives had ever happened before. If they had, what was going on at that time? And if this is a first time, what was he doing that induced stress and that might be mitigated?

But maybe David isn't so different. In doing research for this book, I have uncovered a number of "Davids," men and women of different ages who reported physical symptoms that range from eczema to actually passing out from exhaustion. In every instance, their explanation was that they felt they just had to work at that pace and take on so much. Their brain, their self-talk, said they could power through demands and push aside any physical symptoms. They did not stop, look, and listen. Two people said they were trying to live up to their parents' expectations. Another individual said that rewards had been paramount. And another case study was trying to live up to an unrealistic self-image. It is amazing how our internal self-talk overrides what our body is telling us—if only we would listen!

The price for not stopping might be life-threatening. In 2013, twenty-one-year-old Moritz Erhardt was discovered dead, sprawled across the shower floor and slumped against the door. Erhardt had won a highly competitive summer internship at Bank of America Merrill Lynch in London, but it was a costly victory. An article in *The Guardian* quoted one City intern who told the reporter that, at the time of Erhardt's death, working for more than one hundred hours a week was normal for interns, but despite the pressure, he and the other interns enjoyed the experience. Though Erhardt's cause of death was officially an epileptic seizure, the coroner identified that the underlying problem might have been exhaustion.[1]

In my current research, summer interns in many global financial institutions are still expected to work from 9 a.m. to 2 a.m. Sure, they are paid handsomely for it, but one has to ask, what price is being paid with their body? Goldman Sachs issued an edict in 2015 stating that interns have to stay out of the office from midnight until 9 a.m. Bank of America interns are also told the same and not to work on weekends. As far as I can tell, however, other investment firms do not have such mandates. Rather, it appears that perceived pressure to be seen as one of "the team" pushes individuals to extremes that might be harmful. Perhaps some team members have the stamina of a thoroughbred and can go the distance. But other members might be better suited to a deliberate, slower pace.

### RUN THE RACE BUT AT YOUR OWN PACE

My point is not to single out a specific industry but rather to raise a caution flag. It is possible that some occupations require more "time" than others. What pace suits you? Be aware that your body is a machine that—like all machines— needs to be cleaned, tuned up, oiled, and plugged into an energy source. Machines wear out when used nonstop and so do our bodies.

Arianna Huffington's personal wake-up call came when she went to sleep at her desk and fell to the floor, resulting in a nasty gash over her eye and a broken cheekbone. That experience literally woke her up to write *Thrive: The Third Metric to Redefining Success and Creating a Life of Well-being, Wisdom, and Wonder.*[2] Huffington is now strongly committed to ensuring that her company puts in systems and processes that help employees live well-rounded, healthy lives. Her voice is heard at the yearly World Economic Forum in Davos, Switzerland. As CEO of Thrive Global, her wellness company, Huffington has appeared as a speaker, a panelist, an interviewer, and an interviewee at this annual event that brings together the biggest and most influential leaders found in business, government, and academia.

> The land of burnout is not a place I ever want to go back to.
>
> —ARIANNA HUFFINGTON

But we don't all work for Arianna. You and only you are the first defense in breaking out of a physically unhealthy pattern of life and breaking through to refuel and recharge and align. Consider and *listen* closely to your body. It won't lie to you. Here are some possible physical symptoms: frequent headaches, stomachaches, intestinal issues, and skin eruptions. One of my colleagues was told that her eczema would go away when she listened to what her body was trying to tell her: STOP.

**WHAT IS YOUR SELF-TALK THAT MIGHT
KEEP YOU CHARGING AT FULL SPEED?**

Consider, honestly, what you might be telling yourself.

"I'll be letting people down."

"I'll be seen as a laggard."

"I won't measure up."

"I can rest later."

"I'll never get everything done if I stop now."

"I have too much to do."

*Listen up!* You will *always* have too much to do. In fact, the only person who ever got his work done by Friday was Robinson Crusoe. Imagine how much better your brain will function on rest. You won't have to redo so much or make so many errors. Burnout is not a one-time phenomenon. From personal experience and from listening to so many others, I know that burnout can happen multiple times. But—if you are working on building resiliency, the subsequent flames can be quenched more quickly.

In the Age of Burnout, care of our physical bodies has never been more critical. It's interesting how we can ignore all warning signs until, like Hamza, we collapse. Exhaustion causes us to make mistakes, to redo work, and to lose our focus on what matters. About one-third of Americans are sleeping less than seven hours a night—and some of the people most affected could be the ones responsible for your safety. Among working American adults, health and safety professionals reported the highest rates of insufficient sleep (seven hours or less), according to a recent study published in the *Journal of Community Health*. The study, funded by the pharmaceutical company Merck, analyzed self-reported data from the National Health Interview Survey for more than 150,000 people across the nation over the course of nine years. Researchers found that the percentage of working Americans getting short sleep is on the rise—from 30.9 percent in 2010 to 35.6 percent in 2018.[3] Sleep is not the only concern. Diet and exercise are huge components in our ability to recharge and refuel.

Nothing, I repeat, nothing will help you move more steadily from burnout into breakout and eventual breakthrough than first paying attention to your body. It's your greatest way to gain control when everything else seems out of control. Pay attention to the questions facing this page.

To get to what matters most, we must STOP and pay attention. All of my case studies individuals did not STOP and question if what they were doing really mattered. They kept moving in one direction—convinced that what mattered most was making parents happy, becoming a standout employee, making money, and so on. Until you stop and realize what is happening, what you think really matters might *not*!

It's much like being a wise sailor in the journey we call life. A sailor knows that when the wind shifts, he has to shift. In sailing, course correction is essential. Life also requires course correction. The proverbial wind shifts all the time in our life. To expect a straight course with no deviation is to live in a fairyland and be deeply disappointed. Recall Hamza

# QUESTIONS

Are you getting at least seven hours of sleep? If not, why not? Will the world end if you silence your phone and turn off the television at least thirty minutes before getting into bed? If you are in an occupation with irregular hours (health care, protective services), explore working different shifts at times to have some chance for your body to rest.

Do you exercise at least 30 minutes a day—aerobic activity of any intensity? If not, why not? Push the baby in the stroller. Walk the dog. Park as far as you can from the office building. But move— you get the idea. Sitting for extended periods of time is also dangerous to your health. Google "sitting and health" and you'll uncover reams of articles about the danger of prolonged sitting— from death by cardiovascular disease to cancer. In fact, writing this book has forced me to set a timer on my phone so that I get up and walk every 120 minutes . . . which is actually longer than the recommended extended sitting time.

Are you drinking at least 64 ounces of water a day? Your brain and your body need hydration.

Are you dealing with major health challenges?

and Lin from chapter 2. Their first big experience with burnout came because they maintained one course and never questioned its suitability for their individual lives.

### LEARN FROM OTHERS

For Gen Y Hamza, his *first* burnout, which resulted in passing out in the bathroom, came because he was stretched too thin. As he relayed to me, "I was overwhelmed by the sheer volume of professional priorities, working multiple small jobs, volunteering, and dealing with personal family issues. The weight of the world was too much, and it crushed me."

And yet, Hamza did not change course. He kept sailing in the same direction. "Not only did I not pay attention, I edited my memories such that the event didn't happen. I convinced myself that it was an anomaly and something that really didn't happen because I was in the peak of health. Not only did I move forward with the same intensity, but I trained myself to ignore it because it was so inconsistent with the narrative I was trying to build for myself. The narrative was: 'Hamza's a productive guy. Hamza gets shit done. If you want something done, rely on Hamza.' Had I admitted what happened, it would have prevented me from fulfilling the destiny I *thought* I had—the false notion that hard work will build success all the time."

Like Hamza, Lin Jackson, our Gen Xer, kept sailing in one direction; it took her ten years to collapse. "I went to college at night and worked as a consultant for a French accounting firm during the day. I'd take a two-hour bus ride to Philadelphia while I was reading manuals to try to learn what the firm was asking me to do. On the bus ride back,

I'd do my schoolwork. I ended up with my degree later in the game, got married, and the same week I graduated, I got pregnant."

Pregnancy still did not stop Lin's single-minded direction. "I kept hearing my father's voice telling me to work hard. And I did. On the one hand, I am fortunate because my husband is a stay-at-home dad. On the other hand, that meant I could get up as early as I wanted and travel a lot of the days. I tried to be home with them and have dinner four nights a week. Tried. Not always successful. I used every minute of my commute by making conference calls on this $700 big black car phone (no smart phones yet) and fit in back-to-back meetings. There was no such thing as downtime. I was always working on my Blackberry."

Lin uses a computer term to describe the next few years. "I was constantly multitasking, plus volunteering at church, kid tending, and suddenly, I was thrashing. In computer terms, that means too many tasks and nothing is getting through. No amount of programming will work." Getting more and more tired (yet staying on the same course heading), Lin would come home at 6 p.m., take a nap, and wake up the next morning. At long last, a doctor nailed the issue: adrenal fatigue.

Let's pause here for a moment. Remember, when wind comes up in our lives, we have to shift and align our energies with what matters most at this specific time.

For example, when my sister and her husband were dealing with his stage-three lung cancer, they did not expend a lot of time or energy at work. However, they did not abandon their mutual jobs. In fact, having a form of "work" gave them some respite from this horrifying diagnosis. Emotionally, their attention became focused on each other and the family and friends who gathered for support. They both needed some form of physical relief, and certainly the spiritual dimension of their lives became even more deeply important.

## QUESTIONS

What is this period for you?

Your Ahas?

Please write. As my colleague Sam Horn insists, "Ink it to think it."

## CHAPTER 6

**BREAKOUT**

# YOUR WORK

*It kinda screws things up when you overwork something.*
— JEFF BRIDGES

Time to drill deeper. Recall that breakout creates Ahas when we identify energy-draining thoughts, feelings, and behaviors. With a series of Ahas comes the goal: Breakthrough! Breakthrough is the Ahhhh that aligns our energy so we can focus on what *really* matters most *at this specific stage of our life.*

Remember: Just as there are cycles of the tides and periods of the moon, so too are there periods of our life. What is this period of your life? If it's a period, then no truer words were ever spoken than "this too shall pass."

STOP first. LOOK next. LISTEN deeply.

### EXPLORE THE BIG PICTURE FIRST

Just *write down briefly* the first thoughts that come into your head. Perhaps you're thirty-five, starting a second job, trying to learn the demands of the new job, plus you're in the throes of early parenthood. Perhaps you're forty-eight, recently divorced, a solo-preneur, trying to decide whether to grow the business or sell it, and dealing with aging parents. You get the idea.

Remember, you write to get it right.

### LET'S LOOK AT YOUR WORK

We all work—whether for fee or for free. You might spend time as a community volunteer. You might be going back to school. You might be taking a certification exam. You get the picture. Consider the questions listed. Please write your answers and, as you do, note if there is something that provokes a thought of dismay. You are on to a potential breakout, an Aha. Also, note if there is something that brings a smile to your face. That is also a potential breakout.

Meet Phil Gerbyshak, now the Vice President of Sales Training at Vector Solutions. His burnout came when he was a vice president in IT, back in the days of "command and control."

"I had big-time burnout. The leaders then were almost bending people to their will as opposed to partnering with them. And that was very hard. I was married to my Blackberry at the time and I actually got divorced because of it. She called my Blackberry 'my mistress.' It was very hard."

The divorce struck Phil between the eyes, and his final day on the job affirmed his decision to leave. "My last day was June 10, 2010, when one of my nieces got baptized. Very important to me. But after the baptism, I spent six hours on the phone troubleshooting a problem that went nowhere and my Blackberry went completely dead. I called my boss, the CIO, and asked 'What are we going to do? How are we going to be different?' He said, 'I don't know. That's your problem.' I replied that my last day was Friday and I had just wasted six hours of my life with him."

That experience confirmed Phil's decision. But he lost a wife as a result of not stopping, listening, and looking at what was happening.

Any Ahas? Notice in all these case studies, each person did not *stop*, critically take a deep breath, *look* at what the results of a continued course of action were, and critically *listen* to the wisdom of their body and their partners.

## QUESTIONS

What jumps out as the first thing in your "work" or "job" that either results in an enormous energy drain or possibly reenergizes you?

What are your current projects?

What dominates your "to do" list?

Community involvement?

Volunteering?

Going back to school?

Preparing for a certification?

Paying bills?

Marketing your services?

Traveling for business?

Other items?

What is this period for you?

## CHAPTER 7

BREAKOUT

# YOUR RELATIONSHIPS

*The problem with people is that we're not frogs.*
*Frogs get to eat what bugs them.*

—ANONYMOUS

For years I've taught a class on "Surviving & Thriving with Difficult People." Over the years, participants have brought in stories of many kinds of "difficult people." Sometimes we're related to them by family or by marriage. There are people who keep us steady and others who drive us bonkers and drain our energy. Too much energy drain caused by relationships can lead to the start of burnout. We carry people with us, just as we bring passengers on a sailboat.

STOP first. LOOK next. LISTEN deeply.

*What is this period for you?* For example, there is a different energy demand with a newborn versus handling a teenager. I've often asked audiences to raise their hand if they have teenagers. Hands go up. Next question: "How many of you want to get rid of teenagers?" Most of the hands stay up! Remember, this is a period of time and, as challenging as it can be, this too shall pass.

## QUESTIONS

Right now, who sits with you in your metaphorical sailboat?

What faces do you see? What voices do you hear?

Even more important, whom do you want in your sailboat? Who requires most of your attention?

Who brings joy to life?

Who needs to be tossed overboard?

More and more of us are also finding ourselves caring for aging parents. This is a demanding period of life on so many levels: emotional, physical, and financial. Having cared for my mother in the last six years of her life, and then for two other seniors who had no family, I am well aware of the potential burnout in this situation. I also know that self-care and a support network are vital to survive in this period.

Meet my Boomer buddy, Becky Sansbury, M.Div., a speaker, chaplain, and author of *After the Shock*. Becky experienced her first big burnout at age thirty-five when work and relationship areas collided.

## QUESTIONS

*Thoughts?*

*Aha?*

"I had made the professional decision to take a step back from my career as a professional minister in order to focus on having a family, raising two children, and being a support to my husband, who had taken a huge career step. It took us out of the calm waters of small-town life and thrust us into a Washington, D.C., suburb. I discovered, first of all, that I was much better at managing myself as a professional than I was at being a full-time mother and spouse. I did not have any personal safeguards for how much I put into this new role and assumed I would suddenly become Mary Home-maker and the happy carefree creative mother of the year."

Becky admits to being very unhappy, unpleasant, and never satisfied with how she was handling a colicky baby and a precocious three-and-a-half-year-old. "I was incredibly jealous of my husband's professional accomplishments, all of which took me off track and left me vulnerable to every whim of change and experience, because I had no coping mechanisms at the time to know how to navigate. A year into this Washington, D.C., experiment, my husband had a complete physical breakdown, which led to a mental health breakdown. Now I was trying to add all of his needs into the caregiving load."

Becky continues. "Because of what happened to him, he became another child, and we were suddenly in the midst of an area with no professional guidance. I was doing it all. I became the epitome of someone who could not take care of herself, much less anybody else. So, I did and I did until I came to the point where I could not make good decisions. My health was caving and yet I had three people who had no one else to fall back on other than me."

I thank Becky for her incredibly candid story, which I'll resume later. But first, some Ahas. This was Becky at age thirty-five. Notice that she continued staying the course, even though the winds had shifted, and she was drowning.

## CHAPTER 8

**BREAKOUT**

# YOUR SOUL
# AND YOUR STUFF

*If material things are what you're talking about when you say*
*"I'm blessed," you have no idea about blessings.*

—UNKNOWN

STOP first. LOOK next. LISTEN deeply.

Soul and stuff might seem like a strange juxtaposition, but if you're going to look honestly at aligning energy to what matters most, these two areas deserve attention.

Pierre Teilhard de Chardin proclaimed, "We are not human beings having a spiritual experience. We are spiritual beings having a human experience." A French Jesuit who died in 1955, Teilhard de Chardin was also a paleontologist noted for his expansive worldview. I've never met anyone who disagreed with his statement.

I am constantly reminded in conversations and in research that, whether we are agnostic or evangelical, Buddhist or Jew, we do have a yearning for a spiritual side. This is

> The function of prayer is not to influence God, but rather to change the nature of the one who prays.
>
> —SØREN KIERKEGAARD

the quiet but powerful part of our life that moves us to feed our sense of self, community, and connection to a greater world. We gain energy, I believe, if we take time to realize and express gratitude that we are part of a much larger world. Whether through organized religion, meditation, individual prayer, or communing with nature, our souls yearn for the ability to connect with some "thing" or some "one" that is beyond us and bigger than our human self.

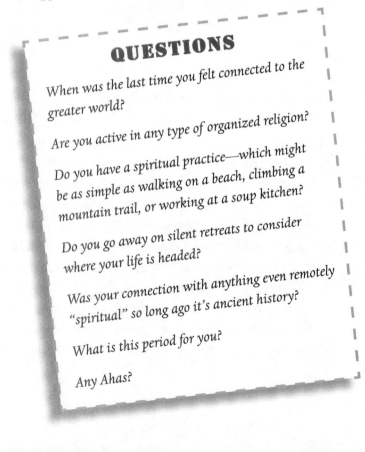

## QUESTIONS

When was the last time you felt connected to the greater world?

Are you active in any type of organized religion?

Do you have a spiritual practice—which might be as simple as walking on a beach, climbing a mountain trail, or working at a soup kitchen?

Do you go away on silent retreats to consider where your life is headed?

Was your connection with anything even remotely "spiritual" so long ago it's ancient history?

What is this period for you?

Any Ahas?

**LET'S TALK ABOUT STUFF**

It is also necessary to consider the relationship of our energy to material choices. We are all surrounded by "things" that we buy and maintain. These things demand our attention and financial wherewithal. It's time for honest reflection on these questions.

## QUESTIONS

What do you have that you currently support? Think in terms of house, car, clothes, education, vacations. (I know. Some of you are laughing. "What vacation?") A roof over your head and food on the table are critical to life. However, filet mignon and 4,000 square feet of roof might not be essential.

What do you need? Given the high cost of living in so many places, you might really need shelter of any kind. You might need a uniform. You might need transportation.

What do you want? "Want" is very different from "need." I recall a conversation with an eighteen-year-old who had just bought tickets to a concert. However, she didn't have money for food. Umm. She had some confusion between "want" and "need."

In the *Divine Comedy*, Dante writes that the deepest part of hell is reserved for those who have what they *want* rather than what they truly *need*.

A quick aside. I had a wonderful conversation with George, a thirty-something who was working two jobs. He put in long hours and yet seemed tireless and happy. No burnout there. When I inquired, he explained that this money would enable him to buy a house for his

**QUESTIONS**

What is this period for you?

Your Aha?

little girls, and he would be able to build them a tree house. He was overjoyed at the thought of what he could provide.

On the flip side, I'll never forget interviewing a captain of industry in his huge office, located at the top of a high-rise in downtown Los Angeles. When I asked him if he was happy, he scowled and said, "I'm as happy as I can be working." He went on to explain that his children were in private schools, the family took exotic vacations, he had a huge house in Beverly Hills, belonged to a couple country clubs, and more. In short, while he didn't evidence what we would call burnout, he certainly seemed to only enjoy talking about his material excesses. Real happiness was missing.

My story: Perhaps it was having a mother who grew up during the Depression. Perhaps it was her incredible frugality, our meals that cost less than $5, and the constant warning to "save for a rainy day." We used to say that she stretched a dollar so far that George Washington (the face on the $1 bill) screamed in pain. Fish was either tuna noodle casserole or fish sticks. *Real* fish was reserved for special occasions. You get the picture. Money was scarce—or so I thought.

To overcome my fear of scarcity, I convinced myself that if I didn't work *really* hard, I'd be a bag woman. (I don't think I am the only woman who expresses this concern. We live longer than men and outliving our resources is a valid concern.) So, in the material part of my life, it wasn't spending that was the issue. It was being afraid to spend on anything! My husband reminds me how afraid I was when we bought our house . . . and, considering we've lived in it for some twenty-eight years, and given the huge cost of housing now in California, it was the smartest move we ever made.

I finally realized how little we actually need when I was given a sleeping porch at a retreat house. All the other bedrooms were taken. The sleeping porch had a smaller than normal twin-size bed, a nightstand, a desk, a lamp, and a rocker. The bathroom was down the hall. No closet. My clothes stayed in my suitcase. I had big windows on two sides, and I could look out to the mountains and hear the birds and night noises. I was content. It was enough: a bed, desk, lamp, windows, and the ability to get a shower and brush my teeth. Enough. Aha! What a concept.

I realize that asking you to think and write about where you find yourself today seems like an added burden to an already burned-out human. But think about and read your answers. Unless I've missed my guess, you are already having some insights about where your life needs alteration, where there are conversations to be had, and where you can make more powerful decisions to recharge and reclaim what matters.

In the remaining chapters, we'll take your breakouts—your Ahas—and weave resiliency mindsets and skillsets into the mix to gain breakthrough—your Ahhhhs. Remember that resiliency is about energy management, managing what we put in our blocks called time. Energy comes from connections. We gain or deplete energy with our connections to our head, heart, hands, and humor. Our goal is to align energy flows by developing practices that refuel, recharge, and reclaim what matters *today*.

The process you just completed is anchoring you in your current reality, your NOW. Eckhart Tolle, the author of *The Power of Now*, captured my attention years ago as I worried about getting enough work, paying bills, and what to do in caring for my mother. As I read his book, sentences popped out at me and I wrote them in my journal. Here are some of the more pertinent thoughts that helped me grasp what was then my current reality and become stronger.

> All fear, unease, worry, tension, anxiety, dread—comes from not what is happening Now but of something that might happen in the future ... forget your life situation. Pay attention to your life. Your life situation exists in time. Your life is Now. The moment your attention turns to Now, you feel a presence, a peace. You no longer look to the future for fulfillment and satisfaction. Therefore, you are not attached to the results. Neither success nor failure has the power to change your inner state of Being. . . .
>
> If there is truly nothing that you can do to change your here and now, and you can't remove yourself from the situation, then accept your here and now totally by dropping all inner resistance. . . . Negativity is totally unnatural. . . . No other life-form on the planet knows negativity. . . . Stay alert, stay present . . . and surrender to the Now. A way will appear.[1]

Years later, I wrote my own version of Now. It might prove helpful to you.

# IN THE NOW

### EILEEN MCDARGH

The day is here upon us. Today is all we've got.
This minute holds eternity, but oh, our minds are fraught
with thoughts of what we should've done, mistakes of
    yesterday
recalling wrongs, reliving deeds and words that went astray.

Or else we go through motions while our thoughts zoom far
    ahead
of things to do, of meetings hence, of possibilities we dread.
We eat our food in hurry. We kiss our loves in haste.
We blink at dawn; we glance at moon.
There is no time to waste.

Our calendar is crammed with future things we have to do.
We make our lists; we see its length. Our day is never through.
And when each year is over, we dismay at all that's passed.
We shake our heads and wonder, "how did time go by so fast?"

We cannot slow the march of time and yet—there is this plan:
If we would live in present now, we'd find a peace at hand.
Be present, fully present in each action that we do.
Stay mindful, fully mindful, of the life around us too.
Let the future be the vision but THIS moment counts—
    and how!
Eternity is in it. May we learn to live in NOW.

# PART 3

# BREAKTHROUGH

## CHAPTER 9

BREAKTHROUGH

# HEAD

## BRAIN BRILLIANCE OR BRAIN BALONEY?

> *The world as we have created it is a process of our thinking.*
> *It cannot be changed without changing our thinking.*
>
> —ALBERT EINSTEIN

Let's pause and consider what you've done. You've identified a general sense of your life. Hopefully, you've drilled down to identify where you are Now and what seem to be triggers for burnout. It's time to look at the positive and negative energy connections you've constructed through your thinking. You've created this burnout baby and now you have to stop, look, and listen to what your brain is saying.

> Mr. Duffy lived a short distance from his body.
>
> —JAMES JOYCE,
> *THE DUBLINERS*

Our brains talk to us. The problem is that, more often than not, the messages are not about the Now but rather about the past or the future. As John Milton wrote in *Paradise Lost*, "The mind is its own place, and in itself can make a

Heaven of Hell, a Hell of Heaven." It's why in the previous chapter I shared the wisdom of Eckhart Tolle. It's a message I need to read frequently—as well as my own poem.

### PAST PARALYSIS: BRAIN BALONEY

Stuck in the past, we regurgitate everything from old wounds and offenses to wanting life to be the way it used to be. I think of this as "past paralysis." Past paralysis rests in the expression "the way we've always done it." It's sneaky and insidious, particularly in organizations, because few ever question *why*. One gentleman was exhausted from part of his job that every three months required him to compile a massive report that was distributed throughout the company. Then someone asked the folks who received it, "Do you read this?" *Few even bothered to open it.* Duh—take that one off the to-do list.

> A stitch in time saves nine but NOT if you've outgrown the pants.
>
> —EILEEN MCDARGH

### STUCK IN OUTMODED THINKING?

Reality check here. Do you speak up when you have identified outmoded practices? Do you encourage your team to identify procedures that waste time and human energy? Are there legacy systems that are considered sacred cows even though they stretch human beings too far? Is everyone on "the team" carrying their fair load? Are you transparent, telling your team *why*? On a personal level, is your energy being drained? Are you stuck because of past grudges, old hurts, or wanting your old life back?

Barbara, a highly respected PhD and an icon in her industry, realized it was time to sell the business she had grown from scratch. But she had not counted on the severe burnout that blazed when she was no longer the CEO. In her thinking, her identity was so merged with her organization that she felt useless and used up. Depression surrounded her life. Sleep became impossible. Going into her office was an exercise in futility. Who was she now???

Barbara's burnout reminded me of Burt, an editor I knew years ago. When his paper was sold, he literally said, "I am a nobody now. As an editor, I had clout and could call anyone. Now I am nothing." Barbara was lucky. A leaking pipe flooded her office and literally destroyed years of her articles, books, and files. It was her wake-up call that she needed to *turn the page* because that was then, and this is now. As for Burt, he disappeared from my radar screen. I can only hope that some proverbial "flood" unleashed an Act II in his life.

### WHAT OUR BRILLIANT BRAINS CAN DO IS ADAPT!

The single word "adaptability" is best described in biological terms as having requisite variety. Simply stated, requisite variety means that the organism with the greatest number of responses to any given situation is the one that survives. You don't have to be the strongest or the smartest to move from burnout to breakthrough. Rather, you have to be the one who will consider *many* options in life and not just remain frozen.

As Charles Darwin insisted: "It is not the strongest of

the species that survives, nor the most intelligent. It is the one that is most adaptable to change." Unfortunately, Einstein was right: our thinking can hold us back. Adaptability begins in the brain, in our head! It's where we begin to quench the burnout flame to refuel, recharge, and reclaim what matters.

### WATCH YOUR WORDS

First—listen to the words we use in our head and then speak out loud. Specifically, listen for the phrase "I have to." Every time we think or say "I have to . . . ," we become mired in quicksand. It says that you have absolutely *no choice*. Wrong. Wrong. Wrong. We always have multiple choices. It's just that we might not like the choices, or we stop with only one alternative. That is not requisite variety.

Viktor E. Frankl, Austrian psychologist and Holocaust survivor, and best known for his book *Man's Search for Meaning*, offered this wisdom:

> Between stimulus and response, there is a space. In that space is our power to choose our response. In our response lies our growth and our freedom. It's not the stimulus that creates the outcome as much as the choice. Although it's often difficult to execute, even in the most dreadful moments, we must remember the responsibility of choice.[1]

Frankl insisted that, even in the horror of a concentration camp, individuals hold the power to choose their response. You do hold the power to build resilience when you begin to train your brain, creating new neural pathways, by getting into the habit of saying "I choose to . . ." And habits take at least twenty-one days to become more hard-wired. If you're like me, it can take even longer.

Trust me. I teach what I need to learn. For example, when I started this book, I told my husband, "I have to write all day." He corrected me and said, "No, you don't. You are choosing to write all day. You can also choose to write for a couple of hours. Or only thirty minutes or . . ." (Isn't it the pits when your very words come back to haunt you—particularly from the mouth of your best beloved?)

Consider requisite variety as a way of responding to your work. There's a difference between a "job" and "work." "Job" is what you do for a paycheck. "Work" is what you do for a life. It is that all-encompassing activity in which time becomes meaningless and you burn on all four burners. As Mark Twain insisted, "The secret of success is making your vocation your vacation." Ideally, your job and your work are the same. That doesn't always happen. It might be that your job allows you the freedom to pursue your work. Or perhaps in this Now, you think you're stuck with "the job." That is not requisite variety.

### EXERCISE A SIGNATURE STRENGTH

What talent or gift could you bring to your "job" that would add joy for you and your colleagues? Achor points out in *The Happiness Advantage* that each time you use a skill you are good at, there's a burst of positivity.[2] He recommends taking a survey to identify your top five "signature strengths." You can take the free survey at http://www.viasurvey.org.

No job is ever ordinary—particularly if one chooses to make it "work." Kahlil Gibran wrote, "Work is love made visible."[3] Here's an example of his words in action.

What if your "job" was in environmental services at a hospital ranked in the top ten in the United States? Environmental services is a cooler name for what the job really is—housekeeping! In a recent engagement to speak to nurses, I found myself mesmerized and smiling at a huge purple elephant painted on a window and at various other art objects tacked to a wall. To my surprise, the art is the work of a young, full-time employee in environmental services who, on her first day of work, noticed a window painted with a colorful pair of giraffes facing each other.

She decided to join the fun. "Art is something that makes people happy because they can relate to it," she said. "People are battling cancer on this floor and it's sad. Instead of always being sad, I wanted to help our patients feel better." With the help of the nursing staff, patients and visitors on the unit now see pinwheels, paper flowers, and new window paintings. This talented housekeeper completes her projects on her breaks. According to the nurse manager on this specific floor, the young woman coordinates art projects for staff, patients, and visitors. She sings to patients, makes waffles for the nurses, and draws this amazing purple elephant on a window, all while keeping the floors spotless. As I learned more about this young woman, I realized she's not a housekeeper—she's a homemaker. She's transformed a job into her work—love made visible!

So what if you are not a latent artist? There are still options to recharge your workplace. Here is the wisdom of Dr. Beverly Kaye, an expert in talent development and engagement and the author of *Love It Don't Leave It*. In her creative best, Kaye has crafted twenty-six ways to get what you want at work.[4] Imagine—twenty-six potential responses that can refuel and recharge your energy. Kaye insists, "You own your career. You are not stuck. Know yourself—what would create your ideal workday? What work accomplishments make you proud? Know your strengths—the big strengths. Ask others how they see you at work. Know your organizations. What are major changes in the industry that are taking place? What are on-the-job challenges and stretch assignments that can help you learn?"

I met Bev in 1984 when she had just completed her first book, *Up Is Not the Only Way*. Her insights then are even more valuable now. Your requisite variety—your ability to find multiple ways of responding to the Now—rests in realizing there are many options that can refuel and recharge your day. Much like climbing a wall, you might find opportunities to move laterally to learn. You might explore testing and researching changes in your current role. Think about seeding your current position with more chances to learn and grow. You'll be astounded with the possibilities.

Managers, here's a very useful tool for you: *Help Them Grow or Watch Them Go*. Beverly Kaye and her co-author Julie Winkle Giulioni have crafted an easy-to-read, brilliant series of career conversations that your organization needs, and employees want.[5] Re-energize your team. These are breakthrough conversations.

Another resource: Consider the Pygmalion effect, which I learned about when I taught elementary school. A team of researchers led by Robert Rosenthal administered intelligence tests to elementary school students.[6] The researchers then told their teachers which students would excel. Sure enough, at the end of the term, those students posted off-the-chart abilities. However, the researchers had lied to the teachers. They had randomly picked names and then informed the teachers that, indeed, these would be their stars! By believing the researchers, the teachers' response altered. The Pygmalion effect shows that, when we believe in another person's potential, it comes to life.

### PRACTICE REVERSE GOAL SETTING

I had just turned thirty and married my amazing husband. I was working in a public relations firm, handling multinational clients. My entire job was to get these clients favorable press. It meant pitching editors, writing press releases, and holding press conferences. The majority of the clients assigned to me were in real estate development. I was good at doing the writing and the pitching, but I was not interested in it. I really disliked what I was doing. My burnout was prompted by the fact that I could not have cared less that some CEO got his picture on the cover of a magazine. I found no joy in organizing the grand opening of a housing tract. Handling the egos of executives and the demands of my company president drained my energy. Yes, burnout.

I felt locked in because neither my husband nor I had

entered our marriage with much financial security. He was a consultant with three children. I had moved to California following a divorce. My possessions fit in the trunk of my Camaro. My sofa came from a yard sale, and my sister gave me her old dishes. You get the picture. In fact, it took Bill and me four months to find a house because it needed to be furnished and have reasonable rent.

My brain was baloney and not brilliant. My connections with my head were draining my energy. But then . . . How vividly I recall having this dream in which I was standing on the edge of a cliff. I heard a voice say, "Jump. I'll catch you."

Startled, I woke up, pushed Bill awake, and announced, "I'm quitting."

His eyes popped open. "What are you going to do?"

"I have no idea," I replied. "But I just can't do this."

"It's okay," he said, patting my arm. "We'll always be all right." (No wonder I love this guy.)

I gave one month's notice and then proceeded to make a list of what I did *not* want—the process of reverse goal setting. In making that list, it was clear that I didn't like the crapshoot of public relations. I wanted work in which I had some control over producing results that made a difference. I could write brochures, annual reports, and my own magazine articles about things that mattered while I explored what I might do.

Within two months of my "freedom," a colleague asked me to craft a training program for adults at the community college. The two-hour class was *How to Write a Business Plan*. I did it and loved the interaction. I had forgotten how much I enjoyed teaching—even though it had been with junior high students in rural Florida. I had designed a few more classes for the college when, out of the blue, associations heard about my work and asked me to come present to them. I came to realize that those initial interactions offered me viewing points I had never considered.

I didn't realize it at the time, but I had a growth mindset and I was working on a happiness advantage. Finding multiple alternatives for the Now can be more than reverse goal setting or reading a book. It also means expanding your thinking by asking someone for help. This requires both humility and vulnerability. You are seeking other viewing points.

### USE YOUR BRAIN TO SEEK HELP WITH A BREAKTHROUGH

Seeking help is what began to pull Becky Sansbury out of her first burnout. "I began to farm out in any form or fashion—as long as it was safe and short term—care for any of the three precious individuals in my life: a toddler, a little girl, and a very ill husband. There were times I simply had to retreat for several hours, half a day, and even one full day. What began happening during that time, almost like a wound that begins to heal from the outer edges into the very raw, torn center, is that I began to have some points of healing and some points to be able to rediscover who I was at that time." Becky's adaptability came when she realized that there were other options to staying home and caring for three individuals. Taking time to rediscover herself was a valuable alternative that supported both her spirit and the family she had created.

Adaptability isn't just a skill for individuals. On a macro scale, consider companies that were once icons of industry. An inability to adapt to changing times and an insistence on staying the course despite changing conditions devastated Kodak, Nokia, Blockbuster, Hitachi, and more. You and I are only smaller than these once-giants of industry. If staying the course is what drains your energy, then it's time to consider alternative actions or, at the very least, to think, "I am choosing to do XYZ because . . ."

### WHEN YOUR BRAIN TURNS TO BALONEY

Let's learn how Hamza developed his adaptability when he hit his second and even more severe burnout. Recall that adaptability (or lack thereof) begins in our brain. Instead of creating connections that energized him, his thoughts zapped his strength. While today, pardon the pun, Hamza understands that denial is not a river in Egypt, in his run-up to 2014, Hamza was continuing his hard-charging take-no-prisoners-and-get-no-sleep work style. He derived any feelings of self-worth from the admiration and adoration of others and the image that he was a productive machine.

"I had started my own digital marketing and consultancy company called Splash Effect. I was also a professional in the Student Affairs Department at Ryerson University in Canada, where I won the Make Your Mark Award for my work as the Digital Community Facilitator, the first position of its kind in North America. It was a coveted, pioneering position and, as a change leader, I was celebrated across the country. I was feeding off the idea that here is this almost mythical position occupied by this hard worker who's just breathing out and not breathing in. I was breathing out in the sense that I was writing e-books, whitepapers, and speaking at conferences, consulting, teaching, but there was no recovery. What happens when we breathe out and don't breathe in? You pass out."

The reality hit him hard when he was sitting, waiting to get his ride for a long-awaited trip to Europe, and he could not get up. "I wanted to get up and just get on that flight but I was physically incapacitated. My body was fighting against my mind. I was just essentially neutered by the reality of my body. I was sick, miserable, and my joints were locked. I was having trouble breathing. It was a total system failure . . . the result of months of chronic stress that went unmanaged, and no amount of rest, relaxation, massages, therapy, or medicine could help. I didn't have the energy to do anything. I was wasting away, festering with negative emotions."

Time became part of his healing, along with his mind, which finally got restless. Hamza wanted to understand what had happened to him. "It was so confusing, I mean the shame of not being able to take the trip, being out of touch with family and friends, withering and wasting away. I was finally prompted to take action—to read everything there is to know about burnout stress and resilience. But first I had to say, 'I can't do this anymore.' It was my brain that nearly sabotaged me and itself. I think the challenge was that this brain of mine was constantly in two places at once. It was in the past. It was in the future. It was never *here*."

I think Hamza lived a short distance from his body.

## THE CURSE OF NEGATIVE SELF-TALK

Let's look at another way our head talk drains our energy and reduces our ability to look at multiple ways to think, feel, and finally recharge and renew.

It's all about RED ANTS!

Red-ant thinking is my term for negativity. It means finding all the worst rather than the potential best, and *nothing* will drain your energy faster and push you into burnout quicker. Some people are highly creative about coming up with "worst-case scenarios." I have a relative who is a master at red-ant thinking. Let's call her Millicent.

My siblings and I were driving with Millicent to see the wonderful autumn colors in New England. Just as we came around the bend of a country road, my sister suddenly shouted, "Stop! I must get a picture of those red and orange trees, that blue sky, and the church steeple."

Susan hopped out of the car, and in a heartbeat Millicent muttered, "Well, I hope she doesn't stand in red ants!"

Huh?!? Red ants?! Do you know how hard it is to even think of that? On her last visit with us, while driving on a winding road in the Hollywood Hills, Millicent observed, "Oh, there must be *lots* of accidents on this road." Susan replied, "I've lived here for more than twenty-five years and have never seen one." Millicent replied, "We're not home yet!"

By the way, if you are a red-ant person, be warned: few people will want to be with you unless they, too, are red-ant folks who find great satisfaction in multiplying negativity.

Find a buddy who agrees to give you a sign (visual or written) when you start down this dark road. This is not to say you can't vent, but put a time limit on it—say sixty seconds. At the end, ask yourself what a positive outcome or response could be. One client came to me complaining about a difficult boss. We brainstormed different responses and communication techniques. I also asked him to come in each week with at least three good things he had noticed about the boss. It was hard at first, but he grudgingly found three things, and then another three. Within a few months, their relationship had changed for the better! What my client did was focus on intelligent optimism.

### THE GIFT OF INTELLIGENT OPTIMISM

The opposite of red-ant thinking is intelligent optimism. Intelligent optimism is looking at one's life and reframing events, people, and activities in a way that offers hope and positivity. Intelligent optimism is a source of creativity. This is not being a Pollyanna or a cockeyed optimist. It is, once again, grounded in seeking requisite variety, which offers alternatives for responding.

> No pessimist ever discovered the secrets of the stars, or sailed to an uncharted land, or opened a new heaven to the human spirit.
>
> —HELEN KELLER

For example, my colleague Jesse moved from Hartford, Connecticut, to Berkeley, California, which has a huge pricing differential in homes. Jesse found a place she wanted, made her best offer, and within forty-eight hours was told that another offer had come in higher than the asking price. Obviously disappointed, Jesse began exploring alternatives

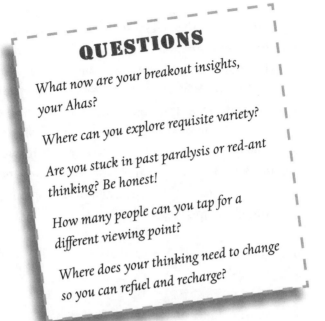

QUESTIONS

What now are your breakout insights, your Ahas?

Where can you explore requisite variety?

Are you stuck in past paralysis or red-ant thinking? Be honest!

How many people can you tap for a different viewing point?

Where does your thinking need to change so you can refuel and recharge?

to her offer. What else might she do? She remembered she had some gold coins in her safety deposit box. She'd throw the coins into the offer. She realized that this was the first house the young couple had ever lived in and the only house their small children knew. She threw in the offer to allow the couple and their kids to come back on a few weekends to enjoy their memories while Jesse stayed someplace else. Lastly, she realized she knew the chief of police in the town the couple were moving to. She offered to introduce them to the police chief, so they'd have some kind of foothold in the area. Bottom line: she got the house.

Listen up: Jesse's breakthrough idea came from reaching out to her network for other options. Refueled with possibilities suggested by that network, Jesse crafted another offer. Remember that seeking insights from others requires humility and vulnerability. Jesse certainly has every reason not to be humble. She has an incredible background: a master's degree from Syracuse University, advanced degrees in psychology and family systems, and a doctorate in organizational development from the University of Massachusetts. Jesse's weekly blog is ranked as one of the top 100 leadership blogs, and *Inc.* magazine lists her as one of the Top 100 Leadership Experts. Yet she needed other viewing points to be optimally adaptable.

## CHAPTER 10

BREAKTHROUGH

# HEART
## POWERFUL OR PITIFUL

*Your heart knows the way.*
*Run in that direction.*
—RUMI

If connections with our brain can either drain our energy or renew it, so too do we have those same connections with our heart.

### THE POWER OF THE HEART

The human heart, with some sixty thousand miles of veins, capillaries, and arteries, is an incredible energy source. In fact, the heart's electrical field is about sixty times greater in amplitude than the electrical activity generated by the brain. We can feel that energy.[1]

Think about a time when you walked into a neighbor's house and you could feel the tension between the spouses or partners. Your heart sensed it. Not your brain. And that negative energy came from their hearts. We now know that the heart talks to the brain. In fact, emotional responses in the heart trigger reactions in the brain.

Dr. Mimi Guarneri, founder and medical director of the Scripps Center for Integrative Medicine, has been an attending physician in cardiovascular disease at Scripps Clinic since 1995. Her book *The Heart Speaks* details the research done by John and Beatrice Lacey in the 1960s and 1970s.[2] The Laceys discovered that the heart was an organ of great intelligence, with its own nervous system, decision-making powers, and connections to the brain. Then, in 1991, Dr. J. Andrew Armour introduced the concept of the "heart brain." His pioneering work demonstrated that the elaborate circuitry of this "little brain" allows it to act independently of the cranial brain—to learn, remember, even to sense and feel. Apparently, the heart has not only its own language but also its own mind.

### THE HEART REMEMBERS AND RESPONDS

Dr. Guarneri's writing also reveals a startling fact. Heart transplant patients may suddenly display unique characteristics and memories that belonged to the heart donor. This fact left me speechless and, as a speaker, that says something! The implication is that we can literally talk to our heart and change emotions and responses from negative to positive, from anxious to calm.

### CHANGING HEART ENERGY INTO EMOTIONAL SELF-MANAGEMENT

Thanks to the work started in 1991 by Doc Childre, founder of the HeartMath Institute, more than twenty-five years of scientific research shows that we can self-regulate the heart's energy and use it to heal our bodies and our lives.[3] The effectiveness of the HeartMath Solution® and its Freeze-Frame® technique in managing mental and emotional responses to events in our life that prompt burnout has been corroborated by more than three hundred peer-reviewed or independent studies. What a breakthrough to realize that by connecting with our positive heart energy, we are building resilience.

The science and the techniques are powerful. Negative emotions lead to a disorder in the autonomic nervous system and produce a chaotic heart rate variability (HRV) pattern that adversely impacts the entire body. The concept is that you freeze the negative emotion in your mind, much as you would freeze a movie frame. You then begin to take deep breaths, replacing the anger, rage, fear—whatever—with thoughts of love and appreciation. It is not voodoo. Positive feelings produce heart-rhythm coherence that can be seen on a scan. As Dr. Guarneri knows, HRV is as important as low cholesterol.

I suspect we're not all that surprised by these findings. In 1943, Antoine de Saint-Exupéry, the French author and pioneering aviator, explained it best in *The Little Prince*: "And now here is my secret, a very simple secret: It is only with the heart that one can see rightly; what is essential is invisible to the eye."[4]

### YOUR HEART AND INTUITION

The heart serves as a source of intuition or internal knowing. How many times have you or I made some error in judgment, only to hear ourselves say later, "I felt it was wrong, but . . ." Our brain overrode our heart. This happens more than we'd like to admit, because it takes courage to listen to our heart. In fact, the word *courage* comes from the French word *coeur*, or heart. In short, our heart connection can be powerful or pitiful.

Think back to Lin, who said that she was like a frog in boiling water because she refused to admit the heat until it was almost too late. Here's more of her story.

"I was pregnant with my first child, and the president of the company I worked for then (a pet food company) wanted to see me in his office. I remember thinking that he was going to count me out because I'm having a baby. Instead he basically said, 'I want you to be the role model for all women to show that women can have it all.' I thought it was real so I literally worked until the day I delivered with my big swollen ankles up on a box under my desk and beside my desk was the intern they hired to get up and walk for me because I couldn't walk."

QUESTIONS

*How about you? What does your gut say?*

*What are your Ahas?*

Think of the courage it would have taken for Lin to say "no." Better still, what if she had found the courage to negotiate what it would mean for her and the company to actually role-model how to successfully and thoughtfully handle pregnancy.

## HEART ENERGY FEEDS OFF
## POSITIVE RELATIONSHIPS

Remember Phil Gerbyshak, the vice president of IT who lost his marriage because his energy was focused solely on his work and his Blackberry? Phil went on to spend nine years as a very successful sales trainer. But success doesn't always equate to happiness and positive energy.

"I burned out having to do everything from target identification to invoicing, to relationship building with a client, to marketing myself. Yes, you can farm some of that out, but it's hard to find someone who could capture my voice. That's when loneliness set it. I was tired of being alone. Being a speaker is very lonely: you fly in, you fly out, and you don't get to see results. You might be responsible for kicking off a transformation but you're not responsible for following through. That was hard on me, because I love results. Being lonely is not the same as being alone. By being lonely, I had no one to bounce ideas off of, to share a meal, to create new programs. Being inside Vector Solutions, I get immediate feedback. I report to a chief sales officer and then I have three or four different business units. Every one of them has people who report to me—143 sales professionals."

Now, the energy of his positive heart connection allows him to touch each one and help them be successful. "I have a lot more now to give than just being a sage on the stage."

He concluded our conversation by noting that in this period of his life he is getting rid of "stuff." "I'm wanting peace, wanting meditative time, finding my Zen, and thus moving to the ocean is important. I've lived in big cities since I was eighteen. The beach will help create that place."

Phil determined what he needed Now. He listened to his heart. Phil is refueled and recharged. His energy is aligned so he can reclaim what matters.

Ahhhh, breakthrough.

### WAYS TO INCREASE HEART ENERGY

The power of heart energy cannot be underestimated. If appreciation, love, contentment, and compassion are emotions that calm the heart, who or what draws these emotions to you?

Cuddling a child, hugging your spouse, grooming your pet, or walking into woods or along a river can all be energy-enhancing activities that refresh and recharge—even in short bursts. Remember, at the core of the *heart* is the word *hear*. Listen carefully. Listen to your heart. It does speak.

## QUESTIONS

Do you receive this energy when you take time to be with people you love?

Are there animals or places that renew your heart?

Any Ahhhhs?

## CHAPTER 11

BREAKTHROUGH

# HANDS

## SET A FENCE OR BE DEFENSELESS

> *It's not enough to be busy. So are the ants.*
> *What are you busy about?*
> —HENRY DAVID THOREAU

It's not enough to work on what your brain says and what your heart intuits. The proverbial rubber meets the road when you *act*. This chapter suggests actions to forestall burnout, to break through unwanted habits, and to build resilience to refuel, recharge, and reclaim what matters. I consider this the equivalent of putting your hand to the shovel and starting to dig away.

### FIRST THINGS FIRST:
### WHERE DO YOU PUT YOUR ENERGY?

We can't begin to control our energy and time if we don't know where it is going. We can't set up boundaries for different parts of our life if we don't realize how many ways we allow, invite, or ignore trespassing actions and people.

We must decide just what of our life's perimeter we need to guard, or at least have a proverbial gate that opens only by invitation. Without that knowledge, it's difficult to get our energy in alignment.

It is time to get busy—purposefully busy and not busy work. Putting your "hand" into motion is essential because challenging and getting Ahas from your thoughts and feelings are not enough to create momentum for a breakthrough. As I have said repeatedly, *"Action is the antidote for anxiety."*

I am going to recommend a series of actions. You decide, at this period in your life, what actions you must take first. I want you to have plenty of breakout thoughts so you can channel your energy where it is needed at this time in your life. I want you to feel a breakthrough—Ahhhh.

First, if you are not really clear on where this precious thing called life (your energy and your time) is going, you might consider a CAT scan. That's my acronym for:

CHECK what claims your time

ASSESS why and how. Is it of value?

TAKE action (what can you amend, avoid, alter, or accept)

Here's how it works. Get a notebook (or use your journal) and make three columns. Label them *time*, *what*, and *who*. For the space of seven days, keep a log from the minute you get up until you go to bed. As you go through your day, briefly write down what you are doing, the amount of time you spend, and who is involved.

Guess what? All activities—for some strange reason—

normally happen in fifteen-minute blocks. It might take you fifteen minutes to take a shower and get dressed. That's .25 on your log. It might take 1.25 hours (seventy-five minutes) to drive to work—while you are probably talking on the phone. Another .5 hour (thirty minutes) to hunt for the email you need to answer, and so on. Okay, I can hear you now: "Say what?! You're nuts, lady. I'm not doing that!" Understand this exercise is optional. But I'll bet that after just three days of doing this, you will find you engage in patterns of behavior that are energy draining, that you have some people in your life who suck you dry, and that you are complicit in allowing and enabling this to happen.

The first time I applied the CAT scan process to my life, I discovered things I had no idea I was doing. For example, I spent a ton of time trying to find a file I needed. Clue: My office really needed organization. I had no idea how much energy / time I was giving to a board position on a nonprofit. When I assessed how much time I was giving, I resigned. I realized that *it was not of value to me for where I was at this point in my life*. I needed to set up a fence, for now, and get out of that activity.

I also had no idea how much time I was spending with an elderly widow who had lost her husband a year or so earlier. Jeanne and her husband had never had any children, so my Bill and I watched out for them. However, his death brought out a mean-spirited streak in her. Nothing I did could satisfy her negativity and fault finding. No, I did not abandon her, *but* I reduced the amount of time I gave her so I could concentrate on my marriage and family. That was a big Aha that lead to an Ahhhh—breakthrough!

### DEVELOP HORSE SENSE—ANOTHER BOUNDARY

Easy to say. Harder to do. Developing horse sense means gaining the ability to say "neigh" or "not now." We are like bobblehead dolls. We say yes to any and all requests and find ourselves fried in the bargain. Grace yourself with the gift of declining requests. Many of us, particularly women, have a hard time saying no. When I've asked audiences why that is, I hear responses like:

"I'll feel guilty."

"It will reflect badly on me."

"There's no one else to do it."

"I can't delegate it to anyone." (Really? Or does this mean "by the time I teach him how to do it, I might as well have done it myself"?)

Our ego gets in the way of setting boundaries. Perhaps we feel important or superior because we can take on so much, because we relish being the "get it done" person. Remember: this thought is what kept Hamza going at a frantic pace.

You have to be able to set boundaries, otherwise the rest of the world is telling you who you are and what you should be doing. You can still be a nice person and set boundaries.

—OPRAH WINFREY

If you are very good at what you do, you will be asked to do more and more. I guarantee, few will know what it really takes to fulfill that request. Consider that by giving the task away, it might be done better. It might develop a new skill in your colleague, your best beloved, or your child. You will have another Aha that can lead to Ahhhh.

Part of boundary setting is putting a fence around the way technology consumes our time and energy. Cal Newport, a professor of computer science at Georgetown University, has written two marvelous books. *Deep Work: Rules for Focused Success in a Distracted World* offers both rational and actionable steps for knowledge workers to focus without distraction.[1] Imagine not having your energy dissipated by a frantic blur of social media, email, and calls. That's how I am trying—not always very successfully—to write this book.

Newport's other book is *Digital Minimalism: Choosing a Focused Life in a Noisy World.*[2] If *Deep Work* is for strictly cognitive efforts, *Digital Minimalism* is for everyday life. Newport relates that the common term he has heard about today's digital life is "exhaustion." Newport calls for digital "decluttering" and—take a deep breath—a thirty-day fast from all

## QUESTIONS

At this point in your life, what might give you more energy?

What matters most in your work?

In your relationships?

In your physical well-being?

And in your spirit?

but essential emails, apps, social media, and the like. That means you don't waste energy on liking Facebook posts, Instagram, or Twitter feeds.

Shocking. Scary. For some, such decluttering might feel like withdrawal pains from a narcotic. I dare you to try it—even for two days. Aha might become an Ahhhh.

### LEARN TO NEGOTIATE ASSIGNMENTS—
### A BIG BOUNDARY SETTER!

Everything we are asked to do is like a three-legged stool: what is to be done; when it is to be done; and what resources can be used. Often one of those things is negotiable, but we don't ask. The request for "right away" might really be "in five days," but we didn't ask. The request for helping at the school play might really be just handing out programs rather than building sets and making costumes. The two-hundred-page report you turned in with footnotes, charts, and graphs might have been handled with a two-page summary. But you didn't ask, "Exactly what do you want in this report?" You get the idea. *Stop* nodding your head. Look. Listen. Then act!

### PRACTICE KNOW, FEEL, DO

This brilliant technique was developed by my colleague Bill Jensen (nicknamed Mr. Simplicity). Specifically, before you convene a meeting, send an email, make a presentation, or leave a voice mail related to work, ask or clarify these three things:

KNOW: What's the one thing I want people to know, understand, learn, or question? Write it out.

FEEL: How do I want people to feel when I am done? Write it out.

DO: What do I want people to do as a direct result of my communication or meeting? Write it out.

I shared this technique with the finance division of a global consumer products company. They did this exercise and . . . breakthrough! I can't tell you the number of managers who jumped up and canceled meetings because they realized these were a waste of time and energy. The other insight was that they had invited the wrong people to the meeting.

If you are on the receiving end of these meetings, emails, and so on, screw up your courage and ask these questions of the person who called the meeting or sent the email. Imagine the energy that can be focused and recharged on what matters!

In Bill's book, *The Simplicity Survival Handbook*, you'll find thirty-two ways to do less and get more done.[3] Then you can refuel, recharge, and reclaim what matters!

Managers, take a clue from Arianna Huffington, founder and CEO of *The Huffington Post*. She has created "Thrive Time" as part of the ordinary workday. This is not about vacations, but rather recognizes that it's better to be proactive about preventing burnout from the start. Specifically, when individuals are putting in extra time, meeting deadlines, going above and beyond, they get to take time off to recover and recharge. It might be taking a few hours, an afternoon, even an entire day. In fact, it's considered a good practice and necessary to keep the organization "thriving." Not taking time off would be a risk.

Consider this. As reported by *Business Insider*, a Microsoft subsidiary in Japan reduced its workweek in the summer by one day, which led to a 40 percent boost in productivity![4] Not only did employees benefit but also the company found it preserved electricity and office resources. Electricity consumption decreased by 23.1 percent, and the number of printed pages decreased by 58.7 percent. This was part of Microsoft's "Work-Life Challenge" trial, which will continue in the winter.

Other companies around the globe are also experimenting with a shorter workweek. A study in 2018 of nearly three thousand workers in eight countries by the Workforce Institute of Kronos and Future Workplace found that most workers said their ideal workweek would be four days or less.

## CHAPTER 12

BREAKTHROUGH

# EXTEND A HAND TO OTHERS AND YOURSELF

*We are hardwired to connect with others.*
*It's what gives purpose and meaning to our lives*
*and without it, there's suffering.*

— BRENÉ BROWN

### CREATE A SUPPORT NETWORK

For Becky Sansbury, this period in her life has her caring for her ninety-six-year-old mother, who lives with her. While her mom doesn't need nursing care, she does require care every day for basic needs, safety, cooking, cleaning, and the aspects of life that allow her to live outside a facility with care and dignity. Short-term memory is also an issue.

But there's more. Becky is also the sole caregiver for her thirty-six-year-old daughter, who has an undiagnosed chronic health condition that has kept her from working. The daughter right now requires complete financial support, emotional support, and some help with day-to-day tasks. Becky says, "I formed a circle of six wise women whom I could trust for loving but honest guidance. I introduced them to each other online (because they don't all live in my town) and gave them permission to talk to each other, talk about me, talk with me, and knew that the most impor-

Ask for help. Not because you are weak but because you want to remain strong.

—LES BROWN

tant thing was that they cared about my well-being. They hold me accountable. They call me when I am faking it."

Becky added that one of these women recently noted that she was not laughing the same way. "She told me that I wasn't taking into account the fact that I was 'on' about eighteen hours a day and that she didn't think I was paying attention to the toll it was taking." Up until that comment, Becky didn't realize that she did not have healthy boundaries in her work as a hospice chaplain and for the demands at home. "I now know there are times to take off the mantle and just be Becky reading a novel." Ahhhh.

For Lin Jackson, support came from her sister when it was time to care for their mother. "You can only imagine the partnership. At some point, we did everything together as we were learning. Then we divided and conquered. She took health care and I took finances when it got more routine. I don't know what somebody does who's an only child."

Lin's point is so valid. I could never have cared for Mom without my amazing sister, Susan, who lives some seventy miles north of me. During that period, I'd accept work only if I knew my sister could come down and cover for me if need be, and I would not leave the United States. We both altered our connections with other parts of our life to care for Mom, because that was what mattered most. Although my business diminished without my regular amount of attention, letting go during this period allowed us both to experience our mother in a more intimate and precious way.

And if you have no sister or brother? Start creating a mutual support group with friends. For you to maintain your resilience, you need the underpinnings of others. You can't wait until you suddenly need help. Make a conscious choice now and put it into action.

> A snowflake is one of God's most fragile creations, but look what they can do when they stick together.
>
> —UNKNOWN

Social support is needed not only in caretaking. It's essential for life! Shawn Achor, author of *The Happiness Advantage*, points out that social support is a far greater predictor of happiness than any other factor.[1] Studies have found that people with strong relationships are less likely to perceive situations as stressful in the first place. When it comes to burnout, individuals who invest in their social support systems are simply better able to thrive under difficult circumstances.

**QUESTIONS**

Who has your back?

How will you nurture these relationships?

### EXTEND YOUR HAND TO OTHERS

You can gain energy when you support others. In fact, you might also refuel and recharge when you offer support to someone before they even ask for it. Think of this as a *random act of kindness*. According to researcher Barbara Fredrickson, loving-kindness gets us away from self-absorption. It releases energy, boosts our immune system, reduces stress, and can generate natural painkillers such as dopamine and serotonin.[2] It is an Aha that can really lead to Ahhhh.

Try it. Pay the tollbooth collector for the car behind you. Start the day with putting the newspaper on the neighbor's front porch. Go visit a friend in her assisted-living facility—even if it is difficult to observe elders in less-than-tiptop shape.

When I made my almost daily visits to Mom in her assisted-living center, I'd call residents by name, give them hugs, and sing for them. It's sad how so many elders are forgotten and abandoned by their families once they are "placed." I admit that my gestures were self-serving, because as stress-inducing as it was to care for Mom in her last six years, I found comfort and joy in making small differences for her and the other residents. My research in writing this book confirmed that I probably also increased my levels of oxytocin, a hormone called the "love" hormone.

### CONTROL THE CONTROLLABLE

Focusing on what we can control can throw us into exhaustion or free us to move into breakthrough. Remember my insistence that we only live in the Now. We can plan for the future, create vision and goals, but we can only execute something *this* day. We can only extend our hands in action *this* day. As you think about your life and work now, do you notice that you are trying to control something over which you—at a basic level—have no control? You now know that you can *choose* your thoughts, feelings, and behaviors and then act accordingly.

I live in earthquake territory, California. I have no control over tectonic plate movements. But I have many choices to consider. I can move (but I choose my Bill over moving). I can get first aid training. I can make my home and car as earthquake-ready as possible: double-hung pictures, bookshelves bolted to walls, plenty of food, water, three kinds of tools and fire extinguishers. I know how to turn off the gas and have loaded plenty of freeze-dried food, canned goods, plastic bags, paper products, surgical gloves, and medical supplies in a large bin beside my house. Plus, I have hard-sole shoes under the bed, a grab-and-go kit for my car, and on it goes. I have an evacuation plan and a communication system for my spread-across-the-country family in the event of a disaster.

I choose where I live and make alterations for that fact. But you don't need a dramatic example like an earthquake to explore where you have control. Look back at your CAT scan.

> I resign as General Manager of the Universe.
>
> —ON A WALL TILE MY SISTER MADE FOR ME

## QUESTIONS

Are you saying "yes" to energy-draining activities or people?

Where are your points of control?

Lin Franklin knows that priorities change as life changes. Her method for getting in control is to put poster paper up on the kitchen wall with painter's tape. Then she uses color-coded stickies to move items around, determining which is urgent, which is important, and what is not urgent or important. "It's a work in progress and it gives me a sense of completion because at the end of the week, I take the completes and throw them away."

### PRACTICE MINDFULNESS

Professor emeritus Jon Kabat-Zinn, founder and former director of the Stress Reduction Clinic at the University of Massachusetts Medical School, is credited with bringing the practice of mindfulness meditation into the mainstream.[3] (See—it's not a California woo-woo thing!) In simplified terms, mindfulness meditation is purposefully stopping, deliberately slowing down, and paying attention to your breath, your emotions, and your body. Remember that burnout is incessantly striving, doing, running, performing, going, going until you are gone. We move so fast, we're often not even aware of where we've been.

Instead, allow yourself to sit quietly, breathing naturally and slowly, just being aware of the present moment. In fact, re-read this last sentence: slowly, deliberately. Can you feel yourself beginning to calm down? Just notice. Just breathe. Simple, um? And healthy.

A review of forty-seven clinical trials found that mindfulness meditation programs show "small improvements in stress/distress and the mental health component of health-related quality of life."[4] Another study found that focusing on the present through the practice of mindfulness can reduce levels of cortisol, the stress hormone.

Mindfulness helps you stay in the Now. It's such a powerful tool that it's practiced by schoolchildren as a way to center them for the day and by CEOs who want to focus and take thoughtful, deliberate decisions. Yunha Kim launched her first start-up in her early twenties and zoomed to the *Forbes* list of the top "30 under 30." But that achievement left her burned out. She became a mindfulness advocate, integrating meditation into her daily routine. From her daily practice of meditation, Yunha ended up developing Simple Habit, the top-rated mindfulness app on the App Store, which has more than two thousand guided meditations, claims more than 2.7 million users, and to date has raised millions in funding.[5]

I'm not sure if you or I will raise millions in funding, but I can guarantee that mindfulness meditation will raise your ability to refuel, recharge, and reclaim what matters Now.

### MOVE IT OR LOSE IT

Your body, that is. Whether it's a mild walk or a vigorous run, yoga classes or spin, Pilates or Spartan burpees, exercise is a superb tool for refueling and recharging. Start small if this is not your "thing." If you will do some form of exercise in the morning, chances are you'll keep it up. The day just seems to get away from us if we wait.

> Exercise to stimulate, not to annihilate. The world wasn't formed in a day, and neither were we. Set small goals and build upon them.
>
> —LEE HANEY

Reward yourself when you exercise—and not with chocolate chip cookies. I got in the habit of putting a sticker on my calendar. Funny, but looking at a paper calendar and seeing a sticker just helps me know I am making progress. Have an exercise buddy if that works. Get a dog you have to walk—though that might add to the burnout load with one more thing to do.

### CAN THE CLUTTER

I remember going into a neighbor's house and seeing a plaque on the wall: "Bless this mess." I chuckled at the time, but now it doesn't seem so funny. Our ability to refuel and recharge is hampered if our physical surroundings are overwhelmed with "stuff."

I'm not talking about Marie Kondo's *Life-Changing Magic of Tidying Up*, although you can certainly benefit from her book and her Netflix program. That kind of decluttering will take time. You picked up this book because you are feeling the flames of burnout now. You're stressed, exhausted, and without energy. What I care about is what you need Now—the single point of focus that will put you in control of what matters most today.

One of my former clients, a meeting planner, asked me to come to her office. She was anxious, overwhelmed, and without energy. As soon as I entered the room, I could see why. Piles of paper were stacked up on almost every available inch of floor space. Pictures were hung askew. And her desk was littered with files. Of course she was overwhelmed. The visual chaos alone created a negative pull on my energy along with hers. I asked her what the single most important assignment was that she needed to work on that day. She rummaged around and pulled out a file.

"Those are the only pieces of paper you can have now on your desk." I carted off all the other piles and put them in boxes that I found. I then placed them in a closet . . . for now. Without the visual clutter, she took a deep breath, smiled, and went to work on the task for that day. Obviously, this was not the end of the story. She subsequently hired a professional organizer to create systems that made sense. But you get the point: take the most immediate small step to gain control over your physical surroundings. It's a breakout Aha. Keep working at it until you feel energy return along with clarity, so you can refuel, recharge, and take care of what matters most. Ahhhh.

> Respect yourself enough to walk away from anything that no longer serves you, grows you, or makes you happy.
>
> —ROBERT TEW

Another colleague was stressed and ruminating over an absence of enough consulting work. I recommended that in addition to her marketing effort, she should go through her basement office and begin to clear out and toss any papers, books, and files that no longer served her. You can't create space for "new" when you are hanging on to old. Weeks later, she reported that she felt a sense of accomplishment and joy by doing that very thing.

Now, do read and/or watch Marie Kondo at your

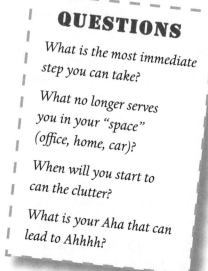

**QUESTIONS**

*What is the most immediate step you can take?*

*What no longer serves you in your "space" (office, home, car)?*

*When will you start to can the clutter?*

*What is your Aha that can lead to Ahhhh?*

convenience. She has some straightforward ideas. It's about minimalism and sorting things by category: giving away and putting away, keeping only those items that bring you joy! But you need relief and refueling Now.

The next two chapters focus on two areas that can help you refuel, recharge, and ultimately reclaim what matters most. These areas build on connecting specifically with the head, heart, and hand because—ultimately—humor and meaning will require all three.

## CHAPTER 13

BREAKTHROUGH

# HUMOR
## THE ENERGY OF PERSPECTIVE

*If I were two-faced, would I be wearing this one?*
— ABRAHAM LINCOLN

Perspective is a particular way of viewing something. Abraham Lincoln was known as a man of humor and storytelling. As he led the United States of America during the Civil War that threatened to tear this country apart, Lincoln was known for remarking that if he did not laugh, he most certainly would cry. His self-deprecating humor threw people off guard in its honesty. It actually helped him develop relationships, disarm some opponents, and cement his reputation as a man of honesty—even about himself. In short, it gave people a very different perspective on this tall, gangly, introverted man who was short on looks but long on laughs. With his short bursts of humor, Lincoln and those around him would be briefly recharged for the difficult work ahead.

Surely, the grave situation Lincoln faced was all the more reason to use some humor. Humor is the opposite of gravity. Gravity pulls things down. In the sixteenth and seventeenth centuries, *levity* was defined as the force that causes things to rise. Levity is the kind of humor that makes life challenges easier. By stepping back and finding the humor in a situation, you can then focus on what really matters. And you can build friendships through shared humor.

Angels can fly because they take themselves lightly.

—G. K. CHESTERTON

### HOW HUMOR CREATES POSITIVE ENERGY

Karyn Buxman is a neurohumorist. Her field of research is understanding the intersection of humor and brain functioning and the resulting increase or decrease of hormones like cortisol (the stress hormone), serotonin (a chemical that regulates happiness and well-being), oxytocin (the love chemical), and dopamine (a chemical that stimulates motivation). She is quick to point out that humor isn't just about laughter; it's also a relationship builder. Victor Borge was right when he insisted, "Humor is the shortest distance between people."

Karyn states, "When we use positive humor—as opposed to sarcasm—the good chemicals are elevated. I define humor as the ability to find amusement that results in smiling, laughing, or feelings of enjoyment. Our challenge is to train our brain to 'see funny,' to develop a way of reframing something so that it reduces the edge of dismay, disappointment, anxiety, and maybe even anger." Karyn believes that humor channels positive energy to build resilience and move from burnout to breakthrough in three primary ways.

"Humor can distract, reframe, and refuel. Even if a situation cannot be altered, there are often parts of it that are not so serious and thus, when spoken or thought about in a humorous way, increase positive chemicals in the brain."

My example: Mom was in hospice for the last seventeen months of her life. Actually, she came off once and then went back on. One minute she was dying, the next moment not. She was up and down so much I called her YoYo Ma. It broke the tension, made us smile. I couldn't change the situation, but we could find something that made us smile.

My friend Gertie told me that when her husband was dying, he told her what he wanted on the funeral wreath at the church door: "Good luck in your new location."

Reframing with humor is another way to get through a challenging situation. Imagine having a company and the product you launch is a dud, a flop! Well, Ben & Jerry's Ice Cream has launched a number of flavors that were duds. Their solution: create a graveyard of unwanted flavors and write something humorous on the tombstone. Here are some of their epitaphs.

PEANUTS! POPCORN!
*Peanuts. Popcorn. Mix 'em in a pot*
*Plop 'em in your ice cream*
*Well—maybe not.*

HOLY CANNOLI
*Now in front of the pearly gates*
*Holy Cannoli sits and waits*
*What brought its ruin, no one knows.*
*Must have been the pistachios.*

Karyn believes you can use external or internal methods to connect with humor. She has humorous items on her smart phone—from funny plays to silly animal videos to funny memes. She has a humor buddy and, when either of them needs a break from stress, they text each other and say, "Send me something funny." She also recommends going to YouTube and typing in "TED" or "TEDx" and "humor."

I've also created a catalogue in my brain of what I call moments of mirth. These are funny stories that I originally wrote in a journal, but I now have purposefully put into my brain. So when I need a distraction from, say, sitting in a dentist's chair, I can pull out a moment of mirth.

I have buddies in Australia who are always finding humorous signs and sending me a photo. I loved the one that said, "Psychic fair—Canceled for unforeseen circumstances." My brother sends me crazy signs, and often they are out in public for the chuckle. Like this one from a church bulletin: "Next Sunday, Mrs. Vinson will be the soloist for the morning service. The pastor will then speak on 'It's a TERRIBLE Experience.'"

Karyn also contends that humor brings perspective to answer the question "What really is important here?" When a car cuts her off on the freeway, rather than stressing, she asks herself, "Did this stop the rotation of the earth?" Now that puts everything in perspective!

In caring for their dying father, Lin and her sister found a way to have comic relief. "We'd laugh over some of the things he said during the day. It was like a rite of passage where every night we knew it was coming up and we'd be able to decompress and get some humor."

In caring for her mother, Becky Sansbury created an evening ritual. "We sit together on the couch, watch a game show but also visit. We watch programs about baby animals. We watch sitcoms from the 1960s and 1970s when life was delightful, and everything could be wrapped up in thirty or sixty minutes. You could walk away feeling good about stuff. And by 10 p.m., there's a plan for laughing about the fact that she has to eat prunes and take her pills. We don't have to go out to seek the experience. It's indeed part of our life now."

If your burnout is prompted by caring for someone, you might gain some ideas here. And we dare not forget the kissing cousin of humor: *play*.

## QUESTIONS

What can you do to create a moment of mirth?

Any laughter Ahas?

### THE VALUE OF PLAY

The opposite of play is not work. According to Stuart Brown, MD, the opposite of play is depression![1] As founder of the National Institute for Play, Brown has spent his career conducting thousands of "play histories" of humans from all walks of life: from Nobel Prize winners and CEOs to serial murderers. (In the latter case, what the murderers had in common: they never played as children!) Humans are hardwired to play, which has implications for social interactions, creativity, brain functioning, and the ever-important resiliency skill—adaptability. When our attachment to work and its responsibilities creates a vacuum for play, depression sets in.

In his seminal book *Play: How It Shapes the Brain, Opens the Imagination, and Invigorates the Soul*, Brown says, "Work and play are like the timbers that keep our house from collapsing down on top of us." Without play, our souls become overburdened, dull, and, frankly, potentially burned out.

Play so you may be serious.

—ANARCHIS

The reason: play is the catalyst for creativity. Creativity allows us to escape the boring and tedious. Break apart the word "recreation" and you discover *re*-create. Innovation and improvisation are cornerstones for finding requisite variety—a critical resiliency skill. When we step off the ordinary and rigidly programmed path, a sense of delight, joy, and wonder arises. As Isaac Asimov said, "The most exciting phrase to hear in science, the one that heralds new discoveries, is not "Eureka! But 'That's funny.'"

But don't think of play as a sandbox for children or the rough-and-tumble world of little boys and girls. By definition, play is purposeless, all-consuming, and fun. Yet as Stuart Brown illustrates, play is anything but trivial. It is a biological drive as integral to our health as sleep or nutrition. We are designed by nature to flourish through play. Play runs the gamut from physical play to mental play, from singing and dancing to social "games" (not video games) and any other activity that is done for the sheer fun of it. Think of this as social investment, creating a place and space for people to enjoy and share something other than "business." It refuels, recharges, and allows individuals to reclaim what matters—the human spirit.

AN ULTIMATE EXAMPLE. I was invited to speak at the corporate headquarters of Ultimate Software in Weston, Florida. Their tagline, "People First," doesn't apply just to customers. The company takes every chance to let employees know they matter—first! And fun is a way to connect. In the Santa Ana, California, office of Ultimate, the UltiPeeps might cavort in the outdoor fountain, have NERF-gun battles, host putting contests on artificial turf, and enjoy a visit from the in-house ice cream cart with free treats. No wonder they are ranked #8 on *Fortune* magazine's 2019 list of the *100 Best Companies to Work For*, having ranked in the top twenty-five on the list since 2012. Ultimate was also named *Fortune's #1 Best Workplace for Millennials* in 2018 for the second consecutive year and #1 on *Fortune's Best Workplaces in Technology*.

SOUTHWEST AIRLINES. Herb Kelleher, founder and former CEO of Southwest Airlines, made play a cultural cornerstone of that organization. From very funny safety announcements on planes to interviewing practices that asked a potential candidate to relay something that was playful or funny in life, Kelleher knew that *play* was essential to keep both employees *and* customers. He told a reporter that the company hires for attitude over expertise, and attitude is found in a sense of humor! Their stock symbol is LUV, and co-workers are known as co-hearts. Although Kelleher died in January of 2019, a culture committee is charged with keeping these values alive, including a Fun-LUVing attitude.

As I write these examples, I am convinced that to grow in resiliency, to refuel, to recharge and keep burnout at bay, play might be the most important work we do.

### LOOK TO CHILDREN FOR PLAY

Becky makes sure she spends at least an hour a week with her five-year-old grandson because *he reminds her how to play*. Interesting that we must be reminded how to play! The school system in Finland is ranked #1 in the world for childhood education by the Organisation for Economic Co-operation and Development, the World Economic Forum, and UNICEF. Finnish educators focus not on standardized tests and numerical assessments but rather on equity, happiness, and joy in learning.[2] They see that the work of a child is to play—and to play outdoors, because when their bodies

## QUESTIONS

If you stopped what you were doing right now and walked in nature, would it refuel, recharge, and refresh your spirit?

What would it take to connect with your head, heart, and hands and take command of where you are at this point of your life?

Where can you find a way to insert humor and play into your day?

What is stopping you?

Do you see ways to gather your Ahas and move to Ahhhh?

are moving, their brains are working. Children are able to concentrate more. They are creative. And school becomes a child's favorite place.

Yikes! Too often we burned-out adults think that play can only happen "when the work is done."

> Play is the exaltation of the possible.
>
> —MARTIN BUBER

Hamza learned otherwise and doesn't wait to play. He now restores his spirit in the outdoors with camping. "I love going into the outdoors, reconnecting with nature, being in forests, near quarries, and taking in the essence of what it means to be a living, breathing organism. To take myself away from the hustle, bustle, and the unnatural nature of a big city and to stare out at vistas creates a feeling of awe and a wonder at the world around us. It subdues my own ego."

**CONCLUSION**

# THE POWER
# OF MEANING

> *Losing your way on a journey is unfortunate.*
> *But, losing the reason for the journey is a fate more cruel.*
>
> — H. G. WELLS

This last chapter is not about your eulogy but rather your legacy. I'm not talking about leaving behind a name on a building because, frankly, that's an ego trip. Rather, what will people say when they *hear* your name? Why are you on this planet?

Remember the age-old story of the two bricklayers. One said he was laying bricks. The other said, "Building a cathedral." In that response we hear a powerful motivation. It's called meaning—doing something that is purposeful beyond immediate gain.

The clearer you can be faithful to that *why*, the more energy you have to live each day. You have a gift, a contribution to make, and, as Kahlil Gibran tells us, "when you work, you fulfill a part of earth's furthest dream, assigned to you when that dream was born." Remember the housekeeper in the hospital who brought her art into the environment and who sang to patients. I believe her *why* is just as important as why the surgeon chooses to work in an operating room.

Thomas H. Lee, MD, Chief Medical Officer for Press Ganey, sought to understand what intrinsic and extrinsic forces create a good doctor and how one can stay in a profession that continues to lose practitioners from stress and burnout. As I read his research in *The Good Doctor*, I was struck by the fact that a sense of purpose and an ability to get outraged on behalf of patients were two of the common characteristics among "good doctors."[1] One doesn't get outraged about a situation unless one cares deeply, along with feeling that one's purpose is to make a contribution f or the better. And for the doctors who became Lee's case studies, the purpose did not appear overnight. They had to also search.

Like the doctors, your *why* might be slowly unfolding by fits and starts, twists and turns. I believe it is uncovered by seeking what brings you joy. Frederick Buechner stated it this way: "The place God calls you is the place where your deep gladness and the world's deep hunger meet."

Phil Gerbyshak, now the VP of sales training at Vector Solutions, believes he is more in alignment with his *why*. "I'm serving more people and making a bigger difference. That's important to me. My grandmother taught me years ago that it's all about the people you serve. It's the purpose they have and a higher purpose that you get to serve. I am totally in line with that. The people I serve are not just the sales team, but we sell and impact police, firefighters, teachers, college professors, architects, engineers, and construction workers. Our education platform helps everyday heroes. We're literally saving lives through the courses we sell."

Phil's deep gladness comes from having multiple ways to use his potential. He concludes, "Potential, and peace and higher purpose. That's pretty cool. That's who I am. More energetic and more at peace than ever." Ahhhh.

Becky, at this stage of her life and as caretaker for both a mother and a daughter, sees a convergence of everything she's been talking, preaching, and writing about. As a hospice chaplain, one of the main comments she heard from patients was "I don't want to feel my life was pointless." She says, "I began to see that the people who thrived in this last stage of life found ways to address their comfort, some degree of control, their community, and their connection to things that had *meaning beyond themselves*. In this stage of my life, caring for my mother and daughter has meaning beyond me. I am the provider and it fills my heart . . . and I also know my self-care is as important as being a provider, so I don't get into burnout." Breakthrough! Ahhhh.

Lin Franklin regards *why* as a complex question with three layers. Her high purpose is to make a difference in the lives of future generations by paying it forward. She not only talks about mentoring and helping other employees but also puts that thought into action. And she has two more layers on her list: her higher purpose is to help her children have strong, healthy lives. And the highest purpose of all: bringing an awareness of and thanks to God.

Hamza, my youngest case study and also my *most* burned out, has come to a place where his *why* is becoming clearer because, as he says, "I'm finally, for the first time in a long time, in control of my priorities as opposed to having my priorities control me. I'm a son, a brother, a partner. Before any professional designations and titles, I'm Hamza, somebody who is an author, somebody who is an educator, somebody who is a speaker." Hamza added another piece of his newly found wisdom: "Burn but not out. Let that be a guiding principle for everything you do in life. There must be a flame of excitement when you find what is a good and timely version of something you wish to do, but keep it integrated with energy expended in wise ways for what matters." Ahhhh.

I believe that Sarah Ban Breathnach in her book *Simple Abundance* describes Hamza's sentiment as authentic success: "Authentic success is knowing that if today were your last day on earth, you could leave without regret. Authentic success is feeling focused and serene when you work, not fragmented. It's knowing that you've done the best that you possibly can, no matter what circumstances you faced; it's knowing in your soul that the best you can do is *all* you can do, and that the best you can do is always enough."[2]

Enough. We will still have days when we put our heads on a pillow and wonder if we were "enough." If we did "enough." "Enough" is not about curing cancer, solving our climate crisis, or achieving world peace. On those days, it's wise to recall the words of Marianne Williamson in her illuminating book *A Return to Love*. "No matter what form our job or activity takes, the content is the same as everyone else's; we're here to minister to the human heart. If we talk to anyone, or see anyone, or even think of anyone, then we have the opportunity to bring more love into the universe. From a waitress to the head of a movie studio, from a crane operator to the president of a nation, there is no one whose job is unimportant to God."[3]

When I recall those words, I think of my beloved brother-in-law, Noam Pitlik. Susan and Noam lost his battle with lung cancer. Noam was an Emmy Award–winning comedy director in Hollywood. If you are old enough, you might recall his television shows: *Barney Miller*, *Taxi*, *Mr. Belvedere*, and more. At the celebration of Noam's life, in an industry that can be known for eating its young alive, I listened to people offering their thoughts. No one said, "He made us a lot of money" or "He won us Emmys." Rather, they talked about how Noam interacted with everyone. He treated everyone—from the lowly wardrobe clerk to the star of the show—with dignity, respect, and compassion. He knew that everyone brought something to the party. Ahhhh. That's meaningful. What a legacy.

### FINAL THOUGHTS

Admiral William H. McRaven gave the commencement speech for the graduating class from the University of Texas at Austin in 2004. The speech went viral and generated a great book.[4] I chuckled when I saw the video of his speech because Mom—who preceded the admiral by decades—wouldn't let us leave for school if we hadn't made our beds. To hear this advice from a Navy Seal gave me a new appreciation for Mom's wisdom.

There are days in which the burnout bogeyman will rear its fire-breathing snout. You can only do what you can do. I like the thought that sometimes, making your bed is the *best* place to start.

If you want to change the world, start off by making your bed. . . . If you make your bed every morning, you will have accomplished the first task of the day. It will give you a small sense of pride, and it will encourage you to do another task and another and another.

—ADMIRAL WILLIAM H. MCRAVEN

I hope that, as you have gone through this book, you've encountered Ahas, insights about the Now of your life and what you can do to create the energy connections to move into breakthrough. Building resilience is a lifelong process, and each time you practice, the ability to refuel, recharge, and reclaim what matters becomes a little easier. Ahhhh.

But reading a book is not enough. Remember, action is the antidote for anxiety. You must stop, look, listen, and then—act. I have discovered that once you commit to taking action, amazing things fall into place and life takes turns you could never have imagined.

Perhaps it is my Scots-Irish heritage that introduced me years ago to the writing of William Hutchison Murray, a

Scottish mountain climber and writer. In his book *The Scottish Himalayan Expedition* he wrote a paragraph that has forever stayed with me:

> Until one is committed, there is hesitancy, the chance to draw back. Concerning all acts of initiative (and creation), there is one elementary truth, the ignorance of which kills countless ideas and splendid plans: that the moment one definitely commits oneself, then Providence moves too. All sorts of things occur to help one that would never otherwise have occurred. A whole stream of events issues from the decision, raising in one's favour all manner of unforeseen incidents and meetings and material assistance, which no man could have dreamed would have come his way. Whatever you can do, or dream you can do, begin it. Boldness has genius, power, and magic in it. Begin it now.[5]

You've stuck with me through reading this book. I believe you know how to breakout and move into breakthrough and align your energy to what matters most! Yes, there will be times in which you must pick yourself up and start again. But each time you grow stronger. Your power to recharge, refuel, and reclaim what matters begins now. Go for it!

> Tell me, what is it you plan to do
> with your one wild and precious life?

—MARY OLIVER,
"THE SUMMER DAY"

# NOTES

### INTRODUCTION. STOP! LOOK! LISTEN!

1. Suzy Frisch, "3 Scientific Links between Handwriting Your Notes and Memory," Redbooth.com, August 3, 2016, https://redbooth.com/blog/handwriting-and-memory (accessed September 12, 2019).

2. Posttraumatic Growth Research Group, "What Is PTG?," https://ptgi.uncc.edu/what-is-ptg (accessed September 13, 2019).

### CHAPTER 1. THE AGE OF BURNOUT

1. Dr. Herbert Freudenberger and Geraldine Richelson, *Burn Out: How to Beat the High Cost of Success* (New York: Bantam Books, 1980), 17.

2. Christina Maslach, *Burnout: The Cost of Caring* (Englewood Cliffs, N.J.: Prentice-Hall, 1982).

3. Wilmar B. Schaufeli, Christina Maslach, and Tadeusz Marek, eds., *Professional Burnout: Recent Developments in Theory and Research*, 1st ed. (Oxford and New York: Routledge Library Editions: Human Resource Management, 1993), 5.

4. The American Institute of Stress, "Workplace Stress: Are You Experiencing Workplace Stress?," https://www.stress.org/workplace-stress (accessed August 12, 2019).

5. Alison Escalante, MD, "The Truth behind Physician Burnout," *Psychology Today*, May 17, 2019, https://www.psychologytoday.com/us/blog/shouldstorm/201905/the-truth-behind-physician-burnout.

6. Savv-E Blog, "What Australian Companies Need to Know about the Cost of Stress in the Workplace," https://www.savv-e.com.au/blog/what-australian-companies-need-to-know-about-the-cost-of-stress-in-the-workplace (accessed September 12, 2019).

7. Emily Reynolds, "The European Union of Burnout," Thrive Global, December 15, 2016, https://thriveglobal.com/stories/the-european-union-of-burnout/ (accessed September 12, 2019).

8. "Work Stress Costs SA R40bn," BusinessReport, October 10, 2016, https://www.iol.co.za/business-report/economy/work-stress-costs-sa-r40bn-2077997 (accessed September 12, 2019).

9. Shai Oster, "Is Work Killing You? In China, Workers Die at Their Desks," Bloomberg, June 30, 2014, https://www.bloomberg.com/news/articles/2014-06-29/is-work-killing-you-in-china-workers-die-at-their-desks (accessed September 12, 2019).

10. Prachi Verma, "Workplace Depressions Taking a Toll on India Inc. Employees," *The Economic Times*, January 22, 2019, https://economictimes.indiatimes.com/jobs/workplace-depression-taking-a-toll-on-india-inc-employees/articleshow/67633549.cms?from=mdr&utm_source=contentofinterest&utm_medium=text&utm_campaign=cppst (accessed September 12, 2019).

11. "Burn-Out an 'Occupational Phenomenon': International Classification of Diseases," World Health Organization, May 28, 2019, https://www.who.int/mental_health/evidence/burn-out/en/ (accessed September 12, 2019).

### CHAPTER 2. WHAT TRIGGERS THE FLAMES?

1. Hamza Khan, *The Burnout Gamble: Achieving More by Beating Burnout and Building Resilience* (Toronto: Hamza Khan, 2017).

2. "How Smart Phones Sabotage Your Brain's Ability to Focus," WSJ Video, May 16, 2019, https://www.wsj.com/video/how-smartphones-sabotage-your-brains-ability-to-focus/72E56EB0-0B92-44BF-9897-08461040E3E8.html (accessed September 12, 2019).

3. Adam Gorlick, "Media Multitaskers Pay Mental Price, Stanford Study Shows," *Stanford News*, August 24, 2009.

4. Kasley Killam, "A Solution for Loneliness," *Scientific American*, May 21, 2019.

5. Dale Archer, MD, "Loneliness and Death," *Psychology Today*, April 23, 2015.

6. Vivek Murthy, "Work and the Loneliness Epidemic: Reducing Isolation at Work Is Good for Business," *Harvard Business Review*, September 27, 2017, https://hbr.org/cover-story/2017/09/work-and-the-loneliness-epidemic (accessed September 12, 2019).

7. Emily Esfahani Smith, *The Power of Meaning: Finding Fulfillment in a World Obsessed with Happiness* (New York: Broadway Books, 2017).

8. Ibid.

### CHAPTER 3. THE ORGANIZATION'S ROLE IN BURNOUT

1. Julia Hobsbawm, "Why Corporate Wellness Programs Fall Short," Strategy Business.com, September 28, 2018, http://strategy-business.com/blog/Why-Corporate-Wellness-Programs-Fall-Short (accessed November 14, 2018).

2. Cary Cooper, Jill Flint-Taylor, and Michael Pearn, *Building Resilience for Success* (Palgrave Macmillan, 2013).

3. Jim Collins, *Good to Great: Why Some Companies Make the Leap and Others Don't* (Harper Business, 2001); and see http://www.JimCollins.com.

4. Thomas H. Lee, MD, *The Good Doctor: What It Means, How to Become One, and How to Remain One* (New York: McGraw-Hill, 2019).

5. Jessie Sholl, "When Employees Define a Company's Culture," *Experience Life*, November 2019.

6. Shawn Achor, *The Happiness Advantage: The Seven Principles of Positive Psychology That Fuel Success and Performance at Work* (New York: Crown Business, 2010).

### CHAPTER 4. THE ROLE OF RESILIENCE

1. Steven M. Southwick and Dennis S. Charney, *Resilience: The Science of Mastering Life's Greatest Challenges* (Cambridge: Cambridge University Press, 2018), 24–25.

2. Carol S. Dweck, PhD, *Mindset: The New Psychology of Success* (New York: Ballantine, 2006).

### CHAPTER 5. YOUR BODY

1. "Bank Intern Moritz Erhardt Died from Epileptic Seizure, Inquest Told," *The Guardian*, November 22, 2013,

https://www.theguardian.com/business/2013/nov/22/moritz-erhardt-merrill-lynch-intern-dead-inquest (accessed September 12, 2019).

2. Arianna Huffington, *Thrive: The Third Metric to Redefining Success and Creating a Life of Well-Being, Wisdom, and Wonder* (New York: Harmony Books, 2015).

3. Grace Hauck, "Study: Third of Americans Sleep Too Little," *USA Today*, November 9, 2019, https://www.usatoday.com/story/news/nation/2019/11/09/sleep-study-americans-sleep-deprived-doctors-healthcare-police/2543777001/ (accessed November 12, 2019).

### CHAPTER 8. YOUR SOUL AND YOUR STUFF

1. Eckhart Tolle, *The Power of Now* (Vancouver, Canada: Namaste Publishing, 1999).

### CHAPTER 9. HEAD: BRAIN BRILLIANCE OR BRAIN BALONEY?

1. Viktor E. Frankl, *Man's Search for Meaning* (Boston: Beacon Press, 2006 edition).

2. Achor, *The Happiness Advantage*.

3. Kahlil Gibran, *The Prophet* (Knopf, 1923).

4. Beverly Kaye and Sharon Jordan-Evans, *Love It Don't Leave It* (San Francisco: Berrett-Koehler Publishers, 1999, 2003).

5. Beverly Kaye and Julie Winkle Giulioni, *Help Them Grow or Watch Them Go* (San Francisco: Berrett-Koehler Publishers, 2012, 2016).

6. Achor, *The Happiness Advantage*.

### CHAPTER 10. HEART: POWERFUL OR PITIFUL

1. "Science of the Heart," *HeartMath Institute*, https://www.heartmath.org/research/science-of-the-heart/energetic-communication/ (accessed November 12, 2019).

2. Mimi Guarneri, MD, FACC, *The Heart Speaks* (New York: Touchstone, 2006).

3. Doc Childre and Howard Martin, *The HeartMath Solution* (San Francisco: HarperCollins, 1999).

4. Antoine de Saint-Exupéry, *The Little Prince* (Boston: Mariner Books, 2000).

### CHAPTER 11. HANDS: SET A FENCE OR BE DEFENSELESS

1. Cal Newport, *Deep Work: Rules for Focused Success in a Distracted World* (United Kingdom: Little, Brown Book Group, 2016).

2. Cal Newport, *Digital Minimalism: Choosing a Focused Life in a Noisy World* (New York: Portfolio, 2019).

3. Bill Jensen, *The Simplicity Survival Handbook* (New York: Basic Books, 2003).

4. Lisa Eadiciccio, "Microsoft Experimented with a 4-Day Workweek, and Productivity Jumped by 40%," *Business Insider*, November 4, 2019, https://www.businessinsider.com/microsoft-4-day-work-week-boosts-productivity-2019-11 (accessed November 10, 2019).

### CHAPTER 12. EXTEND A HAND TO OTHERS AND YOURSELF

1. Achor, *The Happiness Advantage*.

2. Shoba Sreenivasan, PhD, and Linda E. Weinberger, PhD, "Why Random Acts of Kindness Matter to Your

Well-Being," *Psychology Today*, November 16, 2017, https://www.psychologytoday.com/us/blog/emotional-nourishment/201711/why-random-acts-kindness-matter-your-well being (accessed September 12, 2019).

3. "Benefits of Mindfulness," HelpGuide, https://www.helpguide.org/harvard/benefits-of-mindfulness.htm (accessed September 2019).

4. Suzanne Kane, "10 Surprising Health Benefits of Mindfulness Meditation," PsychCentral, July 5, 2018, https://psychcentral.com/blog/10-surprising-health-benefits-of-mindfulness-meditation/ (accessed September 12, 2019).

5. Samantha Walravens and Heather Cabot, "How This CEO Turned Startup Stress into a Brand New Business," *Forbes*, June 24, 2016, https://www.forbes.com/sites/geekgirlrising/2016/06/24/how-this-ceo-turned-startup-stress-into-a-brand-new-business/#5acec6e7f74f (accessed September 14, 2019).

### CHAPTER 13. HUMOR: THE ENERGY OF PERSPECTIVE

1. Stuart Brown, *Play: How It Shapes the Brain, Opens the Imagination, and Invigorates the Soul* (New York: Penguin Random House, 2010).

2. Patrick Butler, "No Grammar Schools, Lots of Play: The Secrets of Europe's Top Education System," *The Guardian*, September 20, 2016, https://www.theguardian.com/education/2016/sep/20/grammar-schools-play-europe-top-education-system-finland-daycare (accessed September 14, 2019).

## CONCLUSION. THE POWER OF MEANING

1. Thomas H. Lee, MD, *The Good Doctor: What It Means, How to Become One, and How to Remain One* (New York: McGraw-Hill, 2019).

2. Sarah Ban Breathnach, *Simple Abundance: A Daybook of Comfort and Joy*, reissue edition (Grand Central Publishing, September 9, 2009).

3. Marianne Williamson, *A Return to Love: Reflections on the Principles of "A Course in Miracles,"* reissue edition (San Francisco: HarperOne, 1996).

4. Admiral William H. McRaven, University of Texas at Austin 2014 Commencement Address, YouTube, May 19, 2014, https://www.youtube.com/watch?v=pxBQLFLei7o (accessed September 12, 2019).

5. W. H. Murray, *The Scottish Himalayan Expedition* (London: J. M. Dent, 1951). The "Goethe couplet" referred to at the end is from an extremely loose translation of Goethe's *Faust* made by John Anster in 1835.

# RESOURCES

**RECOMMENDED READING**

Achor, Shawn. *The Happiness Advantage: The Seven Principles of Positive Psychology That Fuel Success and Performance at Work*. New York: Crown Business, 2010.

Ban Breathnach, Sarah. *Simple Abundance: A Daybook of Comfort and Joy*. Reissue edition. Grand Central Publishing, September 9, 2009.

Brown, Stuart, MD. *Play: How It Shapes the Brain, Opens the Imagination, and Invigorates the Soul*. Penguin Random House, 2010.

Childre, Doc, and Howard Martin. *The HeartMath Solution*. HarperSanFrancisco, 1999.

Citrin, Richard S., and Alan Weiss. *The Resilience Advantage: Stop Managing Stress and Find Your Resilience*. Business Expert Press, 2016.

Cooper, Cary, Jill Flint-Taylor, and Michael Pearn. *Building Resilience for Success: A Resource for Managers and Organizations*. Palgrave Macmillan, 2013.

Duhigg, Charles. *The Power of Habit: Why We Do What We Do in Life and Business*. Random House, 2014.

Dweck, Carol S., PhD. *Mindset: The New Psychology of Success*. Ballentine, 2006.

Guarneri, Mimi, MD, FACC. *The Heart Speaks: A Cardiologist Reveals the Secret Language of Healing.* Touchstone, 2006.

Horn, Sam. *Someday Is Not a Day in the Week: 10 Hacks to Make the Rest of Your Life the Best of Your Life.* St. Martins, 2019.

Huffington, Arianna. *Thrive: The Third Metric to Redefining Success and Creating a Life of Well-Being, Wisdom, and Wonder.* Harmony, 2014, 2015.

Kaye, Beverly, and Sharon Jordan-Evans. *Love It Don't Leave It.* San Francisco: Berrett-Koehler Publishers, 1999, 2003.

Kaye, Beverly, and Julie Winkle Giulioni. *Help Them Grow or Watch Them Go.* San Francisco: Berrett-Koehler Publishers, 2012, 2016.

Khan, Hamza. *The Burnout Gamble: Achieve More by Beating Burnout and Building Resilience.* Tellwell, 2017.

Lee, Thomas H., MD. *The Good Doctor: What It Means, How to Become One, and How to Remain One.* McGraw-Hill, 2019.

McArthur-Blair, Joan, and Jeanie Cockell. *Building Resilience with Appreciative Inquiry.* Berrett-Koehler, 2018.

Newport, Cal. *Deep Work: Rules for Focused Success in a Distracted World.* Grand Central Publishing, 2016.

Newport, Cal. *Digital Minimalism: Choosing a Focused Life in a Noisy World.* Penguin, 2019.

Pink, Daniel. *Drive: The Surprising Truth about What Motivates Us.* New York: Riverhead Books, Penguin Group, 2011.

Sansbury, Becky. *After the Shock: Getting You Back on the Road to Resilience When Crisis Hits You Head On.* Raleigh, N.C.: Real Life Communication, 2015.

Seibert, Al, PhD. *The Resiliency Advantage*. San Francisco: Berrett-Koehler, 2005.

Seppälä, Emma, PhD. *The Happiness Track: How to Apply the Science of Happiness to Accelerate Your Success*. Harper-Collins, 2016.

Smith, Emily Esfahani. *The Power of Meaning: Finding Fulfillment in a World Obsessed with Happiness*. New York: Broadway Books, 2017.

Southwick, Steven, and Dennis Charney. *Resilience: The Science of Mastering Life's Greatest Challenges*. 2nd ed. Cambridge: Cambridge University Press, 2018.

Tolle, Eckhart. *The Power of Now: A Guide to Spiritual Enlightenment*. Namaste Publishing, 1999.

Tuff, Chris. *The Millennial Whisperer: The Practical, Profit-Focused Playbook for Working with and Motivating the World's Largest Generation*. Morgan James Publishing, 2019.

Williamson, Marianne. *A Return to Love*. Reissue edition. San Francisco: HarperOne, 1996.

**ASSESSMENTS**

**Burnout Questionnaire**  Adapted by Michelle Post, MA, LMFT, from American Public Welfare Association, *Public Welfare* 39, no. 1 (1981). https://www.onelegacy.org/docs/BurnoutQuestionnaire_PublicWelfare1981_Modified2013.pdf

**Burnout Questionnaire**  https://barendspsychology.com/burnout-questionnaire/

**Burnout Questionnaire** https://adrenalfatigue.org/burn out-questionnaire/

**Burnout Self-Test** Adapted from MindTools: Essential skills for an excellent career. https://cdn.ymaws.com /www.palibraries.org/resource/collection/9E7F69CE -5257-4353-B71B-905854B5FA6B/Self-CareBurnoutSelf -Test.pdf

**Job Burnout Survey** http://www.secretan.com/tools /assessment-tools/job-burnout-survey/

**Maslach Burnout Toolkit for Human Services** https:// www.mindgarden.com/330-maslach-burnout-toolkit -for-human-services

**McGill Quality of Life Questionnaire** http://www.npcrc .org/files/news/mcgill_quality_of_life.pdf

**MindTools Burnout Self-Test** https://www.mind tools.com/pages/article/newTCS_08.htm

**Physician Burnout Quiz** https://www.surveymonkey .com/r/WHPQWTJ

**Resilience Questionnaire** http://www.trauma informedcareproject.org/resources/RESILIENCE _Questionnaire.pdf

**The Resiliency Quiz—How Resilient Are You? by Al Seibert** http://www.resiliencyquiz.com

**Resiliency Test** https://testyourself.psychtests.com /testid/2121

**Stress and Burnout Questionnaire** http://static1.square
space.com/static/58e2d54de3df28e295f6709c/59233c
6b890b27a16b2b765e/59233c79890b27a16b2b77a0/14
95481465681/Stress-and-Burnout-Questionnaire.pdf
?format=original

**Work-Life Balance Quiz** https://cmha.ca/work-life
-balance-quiz

**World Health Organization Quality of Life Instruments
(WHOQOL-BREF)** https://catalyst.uw.edu/webq
/survey/seaqol/92343

**Your Personal Resiliency Quotient (RQ) Assessment**
https://www.eileenmcdargh.com/pdf/Resiliency%20
Assessment.pdf

# ACKNOWLEDGMENTS

Many thanks to the patience and persistence of my editor, Steve Piersanti. I will admit that there were times when I just wanted to put my head down and cry—thinking I had been clear and he insisted I was not. As the ancient TV show stated, "Father knows best." And he does.

Likewise, the kindness of the Berrett-Koehler staff is always welcome, along with the assistance of many Berrett-Koehler authors, including Susan Fowler, Jesse Lyn Stoner, and Beverly Kaye. Susan, you enlightened me about the process and the payoff. Jesse, you are my social media and blog guru and gave me your insight. Sweet Bev—you are always available for a shoulder, an ear, as well as a heart.

To my operations manager and right hand, Bonnie Davis. I so value your time and talent. I *know* this book would not have seen the light of day without your technical skill. We are a good team.

To Hamza, Becky, Lin, and Phil, thank you for your willingness to be candid and open and allow me into your life. I believe your stories will help many.

And, of course, my precious family—you are what matters most at this time of my life. I love you all.

# INDEX

# ABOUT THE AUTHOR

Since 1980, Eileen McDargh has helped organizations and individuals transform the life of their business and the business of their life through conversations that matter and connections that count. She has become known as a master facilitator, an award-winning author, and an internationally recognized keynoter and executive coach.

Eileen draws upon practical business know-how, life experiences, and years of consulting for major national and international organizations, ranging from global pharmaceuticals to the U.S. armed forces, from health care associations to religious institutions. Her programs are content rich, interactive, provocative, and playful—even downright hilarious.

In 2019, Global Gurus International, a British-based provider of resources for leadership, communication, and sales training, also ranked her *first* as one of the World's Top 30 Communication Professionals following a global survey of 22,000 business professionals.

Eileen's numerous books include:

*Work for a Living & Still Be Free to Live*, the first book to address work/life balance—a topic that placed her as a futurist in this issue.

*The Resilient Spirit*, her second book, is found from South Africa to California and was written as a response to 9/11.

*Talk Ain't Cheap . . . It's Priceless!* serves as a leadership guide for numerous organizations.

*Gifts from the Mountain: Simple Truths for Life's Complexities* won the Benjamin Franklin Gold Award. A training film based on this book earned a Silver Telly, the highest award for commercial productions.

*My Get Up and Go Got Up & Went* offers succinct insights in an easy-to-read fashion for recharging and renewing human energy.

*Your Resiliency GPS: A Guide for Growing through Life and Work* offers a path for finding your GPS (growth positioning strategies) through recalculating questions.

As a business author and commentator, Eileen has appeared on network news, on radio programs, in business journals, and in major metropolitan newspapers.

Eileen is a certified speaking professional (CSP), and her election into the CPAE Speaker Hall of Fame places her among the top 3 percent of speakers in the United States. She is also the CEO (Chief Energy Officer) of The Resiliency Group. In addition, she is listed as a recommended expert through the Sloan Work and Family Researchers Network, now headquartered at the University of Pennsylvania.

You can reach Eileen at:

Twitter: @macdarling

LinkedIn: https://www.linkedin.com/in/eileenmcdargh

Facebook: https://www.facebook.com/pages/Professional
-Speaker-Eileen-McDargh-CSP-CPAE/405748766188727

Website: www.theresiliencygroup.com

Email: Eileen@eileenmcdargh.com

## ONE FINAL THOUGHT FROM EILEEN

I invite you to share with me your Ahas and Ahhhhs. Look for a special page on our website at https://www.eileenmcdargh.com/burnout. You'll find updated resources, articles, and a place for you to share your story and learn from others. Who knows, I might even form small Breakthrough chat groups. Make sure you sign up to receive The Resiliency Report, too.

Berrett-Koehler Discussion Guide

# BK Burnout to Breakthrough

Building Resilience to Refuel, Recharge,
and Reclaim What Matters

When is a book more than a book? Answer: when it becomes a
conversation! In exploring this entire issue of moving from burnout to breakthrough, it became clear that a lack of talking about
what matters most holds us back from discovering different ways
to respond, from creating new relationships, and from finding a
compassionate community of individuals in similar situations.

I have asked many questions in this book, some of which probably evoked a strong reaction and others you may have decided to
leave unanswered. While the book's primary emphasis is on your
individual life, I felt compelled to include some organizational
considerations. Thus, this study guide has two sections: one for a
discussion group focusing on the members' individual lives, and
the other for a group focusing on an organization.

## Individual Study Guide

1.  What prompted you to pick up this guide?


2.  What case study did you resonate with the most—Hamza,
Lin, Becky, or Phil? Why?


3.  What triggers the flames of burnout in you? (You can have
more than what are listed in chapter 2.)


4.  What would be the "low-hanging fruit" that you could get
to begin to refuel and reclaim your life? Whose support do you
need? When will you begin?


5.  What area poses the greater challenge for you? Ask the
group for their ideas.

6.    In considering the Now of your life, what requires the most energy? Given that energy demand, what can you do to recharge yourself?

7.    What is one breakout idea you've gotten in how you think about your situation?

8.    Who or what brings joy to your heart? How often do you have that encounter? How can you improve that heart connection?

9.    Where do you need to set boundaries? What's holding you back if you are not doing it?

10.  When was the last time you did something for fun? What do you do that you consider play?

11.  What are at least two resilience skills you are going to practice? If you wish, can you get a burnout buddy and check in with each other?

12.  What gives your life meaning? If you can't figure out what matters most, ask at least six people to answer this question and email you the answers.
    Please complete this:
    __[Your name]__ is the best at _____.
    I think _[your name]_ makes a difference when

    _____.

13.  Free-for-all: What do you want to talk about?

# Organizational Discussion Guide

1.   What role do you play in the organization and what are your primary responsibilities?


2.   How would you describe the workload? Always in overload? Just about right? Anything else?


3.   When you read chapter 3, are there areas in which the organization could improve? Where do you have a sphere of influence over those areas?


4.   What would it take to begin a GROSS (Get Rid of Stupid Stuff) initiative? What's holding you back from starting?


5.   What in your work provides meaning? What brings you joy?


6.   How do you "play" within the work setting? (Remember, even in a cancer hospital, housekeeping and nurses found a way to add some light and fun.)


7.   What would it take for you to practice "digital minimalism"?


8.   Feeling heard, understood, and served is critical in all relationships. If you work with or manage others, how would they assess your ability to listen, understand, and respond?


9.   Hard question: What would it take for the organization to capture your head, heart, and spirit? And if it already does, please tell others about it.


10.   Free-for-all: What do you want to talk about?

Also by Eileen McDargh

# Gifts from the Mountain
## Simple Truths for Life's Complexities

Whether you are a world-weary worker juggling the demands of a hectic life or a seeker of soul-satisfying experiences, this deceptively simple book is your key to refresh, renew, rethink, and recharge. From an unexpectedly arduous backpacking trip, Eileen McDargh discovers truths from the experience. Deep in grime, grit, and grace-filled mornings, she finds insights for business, for relationships, for family, for life, and for the soul. Illustrated with stunning watercolor paintings, *Gifts from the Mountain* helps you pay attention to the process of life and take joy in the journey.

Hardcover, 120 pages, ISBN 978-1-57675-469-6
Digital PDF, ISBN 978-1-57675-543-3
Digital ePub, ISBN 978-1-60994-430-8
Digital Kindle, ISBN 978-1-60994-659-3

BK  Berrett–Koehler Publishers, Inc.
*www.bkconnection.com*                    **800.929.2929**

# Berrett–Koehler
## Publishers

**Berrett-Koehler** is an independent publisher dedicated to an ambitious mission: *Connecting people and ideas to create a world that works for all.*

Our publications span many formats, including print, digital, audio, and video. We also offer online resources, training, and gatherings. And we will continue expanding our products and services to advance our mission.

We believe that the solutions to the world's problems will come from all of us, working at all levels: in our society, in our organizations, and in our own lives. Our publications and resources offer pathways to creating a more just, equitable, and sustainable society. They help people make their organizations more humane, democratic, diverse, and effective (and we don't think there's any contradiction there). And they guide people in creating positive change in their own lives and aligning their personal practices with their aspirations for a better world.

And we strive to practice what we preach through what we call "The BK Way." At the core of this approach is *stewardship,* a deep sense of responsibility to administer the company for the benefit of all of our stakeholder groups, including authors, customers, employees, investors, service providers, sales partners, and the communities and environment around us. Everything we do is built around stewardship and our other core values of *quality, partnership, inclusion,* and *sustainability.*

This is why Berrett-Koehler is the first book publishing company to be both a B Corporation (a rigorous certification) and a benefit corporation (a for-profit legal status), which together require us to adhere to the highest standards for corporate, social, and environmental performance. And it is why we have instituted many pioneering practices (which you can learn about at www.bkconnection.com), including the Berrett-Koehler Constitution, the Bill of Rights and Responsibilities for BK Authors, and our unique Author Days.

We are grateful to our readers, authors, and other friends who are supporting our mission. We ask you to share with us examples of how BK publications and resources are making a difference in your lives, organizations, and communities at www.bkconnection.com/impact.

Dear reader,

Thank you for picking up this book and welcome to the worldwide BK community! You're joining a special group of people who have come together to create positive change in their lives, organizations, and communities.

## What's BK all about?

Our mission is to connect people and ideas to create a world that works for all.

Why? Our communities, organizations, and lives get bogged down by old paradigms of self-interest, exclusion, hierarchy, and privilege. But we believe that can change. That's why we seek the leading experts on these challenges—and share their actionable ideas with you.

## A welcome gift

To help you get started, we'd like to offer you a **free copy** of one of our bestselling ebooks:

### www.bkconnection.com/welcome

When you claim your **free ebook**, you'll also be subscribed to our blog.

## Our freshest insights

Access the best new tools and ideas for leaders at all levels on our blog at ideas.bkconnection.com.

Sincerely,

Your friends at Berrett-Koehler

Certified

Corporation